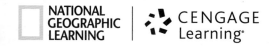

OUTCOMES

ADVANCED

STUDENT'S BOOK

HUGH DELLAR

ANDREW WALKLEY

Split Edition A

Contents 3

Split Edition B

9 WORK

- describe what people do at work
- signal that you are making deductions
- discuss different experiences of work
- talk about terms and conditions of employment
- discuss issues related to dismissal and tribunals

10 HEALTH AND ILLNESS

- describe different medical and surgical procedures
- use vague language
- discuss different approaches to medicine
- describe things the mind and body do
- discuss issues doctors face

VIDEO 5: The cat who ate needles   REVIEW 5   WRITING 5: Covering letters

11 PLAY

- talk about sports you watch or do
- recognise and use irony
- discuss issues around gaming
- link ideas within and across sentences
- discuss and use playful language

12 HISTORY

- describe some of the key events in people's lives
- use similes to make descriptions more interesting
- give better presentations
- ask contextualised questions after presentations
- discuss important historical events
- present and debate arguments and theories

VIDEO 6: The sword Excalibur   REVIEW 6   WRITING 6: Magazine articles

13 NEWS AND THE MEDIA

- understand news stories better
- comment on news stories
- recognise and use rhetorical questions
- discuss the issue of celebrity and the media
- report what people said

14 BUSINESS AND ECONOMICS

- discuss different aspects of running a company
- talk about how your business is doing
- network and make small talk
- discuss crime, banks and economics
- use some loanwords
- take minutes and take part in meetings

VIDEO 7: Counterfeit strategy   REVIEW 7   WRITING 7: Applying for funding page 162

15 TRENDS

- describe clothes and hairstyles
- repair misunderstandings
- give opinions on style
- discuss trends
- use some snowclones
- discuss the fashion industry and its impact
- define yourself in different ways

16 DANGER AND RISK

- describe accidents and injuries
- understand and use a range of interjections
- talk about laws and regulations
- discuss compensation culture
- talk and think critically about texts
- discuss the pros and cons of Internet use

VIDEO 8: Long neck women   REVIEW 8   WRITING 8: Giving information

Contents   **5**

1

Housing developments in West Palm Beach, Florida

IN THIS UNIT YOU LEARN HOW TO:

- describe different aspects of cities and city life
- add interest to stories by emphasising and exaggerating
- reinforce and exemplify points you've made
- talk about urban problems and how to tackle them
- talk about changes in urban areas
- tell stories and urban myths

SPEAKING

1 Work in groups. Look at the photo. Make a list of as many advantages and drawbacks of living in this place as you can think of.

2 Work in pairs. Discuss to what degree you think each adjective would apply to West Palm Beach. Explain your ideas.

dull	well-run	congested	spotless
chaotic	run-down	sprawling	hot and humid
compact	affluent	vibrant	safe and secure
polluted			

3 Would you like to live in a place like this? Why? / Why not?

CITIES

A REAL BUZZ ABOUT THE PLACE

VOCABULARY City life

1 Check you understand the words and phrases in bold in the sentences below. Then put these words into the correct place in the sentences. The first one is done for you.

| ~~springing up~~ | showing off | choke | condemned |
| muggings | smoothly | crawl | dropping |

springing up

1 There are new businesses/all over the place. There's a real **buzz** about the place.

2 The **crime rate** is pretty high. There are a lot of and **shootings**.

3 There's a big **network of buses and trams** and it all runs very.

4 The **smog** is awful – you have to wear a mask or you'd on the **fumes**.

5 The cars just along most of the time – you **might as well** walk.

6 There's a lot of **conspicuous consumption** with people their wealth.

7 There's not a **trace** of litter anywhere. Apparently, you can **get fined heavily** for it.

8 The area is a **slum**. A lot of buildings should just be and rebuilt.

2 Work in pairs. Answer the questions.

1 Which adjectives from Exercise 2 on page 7 would you use to describe the places in Exercise 1? How would you say the opposites?

2 What other things might give a place a buzz?

3 What else might you choke on?

4 What are examples of conspicuous consumption?

LISTENING

3 ▶ **1** Listen to two conversations about cities. List the good and bad things you hear about each place.

4 Work in pairs. Compare your ideas. What cities do you think the speakers could be describing? Why? Which place would you rather live in? Why?

5 ▶ **1** Listen again and complete the sentences.

Conversation 1

1 It's really wild. It _____, actually.

2 We went out with these people and _____ at about four in the morning.

3 Actually, that was _____, the congestion.

4 Honestly, you walk out of your hotel and _____ this thick wall of heat.

5 It does _____ but, as I say, it just has a real buzz.

Conversation 2

6 It is, if you like _____.

7 It's more lively. There's _____, you know.

8 So you wouldn't _____ to live there?

9 Don't _____, it is a good place to live if you're bringing up kids.

10 So if I _____, I might move back. It's just not what I want right now.

6 Work in groups. Discuss the questions.

- What places, people, etc. have taken you by surprise?

- Have you ever been out till four? Where? When?

- What drawbacks are there to the place you live in?

- What 'scenes' are there where you live?

- Where's a good place to settle down in your country / region? Why?

UNDERSTANDING VOCABULARY

Emphasising and exaggerating

We often use particular vocabulary and patterns to emphasise how we feel or to make an experience sound more interesting. For example, we use:

- repetition: **really, really** vibrant / **loads and loads** of people / see for **miles and miles**

- intensifying adverbs: **unbearably** humid / **incredibly** lively

- 'extreme' words that include the meaning of 'very': packed / spotless / crawl / stink

- expressions with like: it's like hitting this thick wall of heat

7 Work in pairs. Do the following:

1 List four other intensifying adverbs.

2 List six other 'extreme' adjectives or verbs.

3 Decide in what situations people might say the following like expressions.
   - It was like being at a rock concert.
   - It was like living in a war zone.
   - It's like Buckingham Palace.
   - It was like the Arctic in there.
   - It's like talking to a brick wall.

8 With your partner, rewrite these sentences to make them more interesting. Try to use all the different patterns in the box above.

1 *It's an absolutely enormous city.*

1 It's a big city.

2 They're doing a lot of building work.

3 The city's a bit run-down.

4 It's not very expensive there.

5 Some parts of the city are quite dangerous.

6 It's quite interesting.

DEVELOPING CONVERSATIONS

Reinforcing and exemplifying a point

When we emphasise or exaggerate, the listener may question us using Really?, Yeah?, etc. We often respond by giving an example. Notice the adverbs we often use to reinforce the truth of what we're saying.

B: ... the nightlife is **totally insane**.

A: **Really**?

B: **Honestly**. We went out with these people and ended up in a place at about four in the morning and it was **absolutely packed**.

A: **Yeah**?

B: **Seriously**. You **literally couldn't move**.

9 Match the sentences (1–5) to the examples (a–e).

1 The place is like a war zone.

2 The place is absolutely spotless.

3 The way people drive is insane.

4 We were staying in a really, really posh area.

5 There's a real buzz about the place.

a They race along the main roads at about 100 miles an hour.

b There isn't a trace of litter or chewing gum on the pavements.

c It was like Beverly Hills. I felt a bit conspicuous walking around there.

d There's a huge music scene. There are loads of venues springing up.

e There's so much crime and hundreds of places have been condemned.

10 Use the sentences and examples in Exercise 9 to have conversations. Add words like *honestly*, *seriously* and *literally* where appropriate.

A: *The place was like a war zone.*

B: *Really?*

A: *Honestly. There's so much crime and literally hundreds of places have been condemned.*

CONVERSATION PRACTICE

11 Write the names of two cities you have been to. Make notes about aspects of the cities and think of at least one thing that happened to you in each city. Use as much language from this lesson as you can.

12 Work in pairs. Have conversations about your chosen cities. Start with *Have you been to ...?* Keep the conversation going by asking questions to get more details or by using comments like *Really?* or *Yeah?*

📹 1 To watch the video and do the activities, see the DVD ROM.

URBAN RENEWAL

READING

1 Work in groups. Discuss the questions.

- What effects do you think the following can have on a city? How serious are they?
- Which three things are of greatest concern where you live and which is of least concern? Why?

an economic downturn	a hurricane	an armed conflict
an earthquake	flooding	a high crime rate
severe pollution	terrorism	a huge fire

2 Work with the same group. You are going to read about a city and how it was affected by one or more of the problems in Exercise 1. Find out what happened.

Group A: read the text in File 1 on page 95.

Group B: read the text in File 2 on page 96.

Group C: read the text in File 3 on page 101.

3 With a person from your group, do the following:

1 Compare what you understood and what you think of the story.

2 Discuss what you learnt about the city.

3 Check you understand the phrases in bold – and try to remember them.

4 Make new groups: a Student A, B and C. Close your books. Tell each other about the cities you read about, using some of the words in bold that you learnt. Decide what similarities there are between the three cities.

5 With your group, decide which city each sentence refers to: Bilbao, Bogota or Manchester. Look back at the texts if you need to.

1 Some other cities have unsuccessfully tried to copy what it did.

2 The government forced people to sell something.

3 Sport has played a role in the city's redevelopment.

4 Some of the changes were paid for by motorists.

5 It has a more diverse economy than it did in the past.

6 It has aimed to create a child-friendly environment.

7 The changes made it better able to survive a second downturn.

8 A bad event turned out to be fortunate.

6 With your group, discuss the questions.

- Which of the cities you read about has the most interesting story? Why?
- Are there comparable cities in your country? In what ways are they similar / different?
- How child-friendly is your city?
- What cities in your country have new iconic buildings?
- Why do you think some redevelopment projects fail?
- Do you think hosting sports events is good for a city?

Bilbao

Bogota

VOCABULARY Recovery and change

7 Replace the words in italics with the correct form of these verbs. Then decide which of the synonyms are more common in academic / written English.

undergo	flourish	pour	be neglected
impose	demolish	soar	initiate

1 The city has *gone through* huge changes in recent years – not entirely for the better.

2 The government will have *invested* £3 billion into the transport system by the end of this parliament.

3 The slums were *knocked down* to make way for a golf course and the inhabitants were re-housed nearby.

4 The previous mayor *set out* an ambitious plan to develop the city centre, but it's run into financial difficulties and the new mayor has cancelled the project.

5 The whole area has *become run-down* and the council has managed to secure EU funding to halt the decline.

6 The city has managed to attract a lot of inward investment and businesses are springing up and *doing very well*.

7 Crime had *gone up a lot* in the 1980s and the mayor's zero-tolerance policy was credited with reversing the trend.

8 In order to ease congestion, the government *brought in* restrictions on car use.

8 Work in pairs. Give one example of each of the following:

1 a place or institution that has undergone big changes

2 a place or section of society that has been neglected

3 a plan or strategy the government has initiated

4 someone or something that is flourishing

5 something the government has poured money into

GRAMMAR

Perfect forms

Perfect forms use a form of *have* + past participle. Passive perfect forms use a form of *have* + *been* + past participle. Primarily, perfect forms emphasise that something happened or started before another event or point in time.

9 Work in pairs. Complete the sentences from the texts with the correct perfect form of the verbs. Decide what time or event each one happened before.

1 Since its completion in 1997, the Guggenheim Museum in Bilbao, the capital of the Basque region of northern Spain, _____ one of the most famous buildings in the world. (become)

2 There _____ some voices of opposition that suggest the process did not benefit the working-class people ... (be)

3 The slum _____ effectively _____ a barrier between the affluent north and the more deprived south of the city. (create)

4 Up until the early 80s, Bilbao _____ by steel plants and shipbuilding. (dominate)

5 If other mayors _____ the city's finances before him ... the changes wouldn't have been so successful. (not / secure)

6 If we ever achieve a successful city for children, we _____ the perfect city for all citizens. (build)

7 Other cities trying to replicate the so-called 'Guggenheim effect' _____ because they didn't take up the other strands of Bilbao's regeneration project. (fail)

8 _____ one space, Peñalosa's administration then expropriated the land of a private country club. (clear)

Ⓖ Check your ideas on page 86 and do Exercise 1.

10 Work in pairs. Discuss the questions.

* How has your city changed in the last few years?

* How do you think your city or country will have changed in ten years' time? Why?

* What are the two most important events in your city's / country's history? Why?

* Can you think of any places that have suffered any of the situations or events in Exercise 1? What happened?

Ⓖ For further practice, see Exercise 2 on page 86.

SPEAKING

11 Work in groups. You are going to decide how to spend some funding on a town called Oldbury. First read the information and the ideas on how to spend the money in File 4 on page 96. Then put the ideas in order of priority and decide how much should be spent on each idea and an approximate timescale for change.

12 Write a short pitch for your proposal to present to the class. Explain the reasons for your choices, the timescale for the different strands and what the outcomes will be.

Manchester

URBAN TALES

SPEAKING

1 **Work in groups. Look at the comments below, then discuss the questions.**

- Have you heard about any of these stories before?
- Which stories would you find most / least interesting to talk about? Why?
- What connection might there be between the six comments?

> Did you see that thing about Google Street View capturing a murder in Edinburgh?

> In any big city, you're never more than two metres from a rat.

> I read somewhere that we only use 10% of our brain capacity.

> Did you know that Walt Disney had his body frozen after he died?

> I heard somewhere that they think lemon peel can cure cancer.

> I heard they've spotted these huge alligators in the sewers under New York.

READING

2 **Read this article about a similar story. Find out:**

1 what the story is and what impact it had in New Orleans.

2 what's known about the roots of the story and how it spread.

3 what connects this story to the six comments in Exercise 1.

BUYING INTO THE MYTH

In early 1997, as the city of New Orleans was busy getting ready for its annual Mardi Gras carnival, an email entitled 'Travellers beware' went viral, **sparking** hundreds of calls to the local police department, who felt **compelled** to issue an official statement designed to **calm** public fears.

The email claimed that an organised gang was planning to **drug** visitors to the city, surgically remove their kidneys and sell them on the black market. Now, you may well be thinking this story sounds familiar. If so, that's because versions of it have been around for over three decades now. Back in the 1980s, Guatemala was **gripped** by stories of Americans kidnapping local children and harvesting their organs. By the early 1990s, there were stories in the States about Latino women tempting American men to a similar fate, and before long the idea appeared in TV dramas and movies – and variations started to appear all over the world.

One thing that **unites** all these stories – and others like them – is that no hard evidence exists of them ever having occurred. These urban myths apparently **emerge** from nowhere and take on a life of their own. This **raises** interesting questions about why we continue to share them and, on occasion, even fall for them!

Festivities in the streets of New Orleans

3 Work in pairs. Discuss what you think the words in bold in the article mean. Then use the words in bold to complete each group of phrases below.

1 ~ the issue at the meeting / ~ fears / ~ doubts about ...

2 be ~ to appear as a witness / feel ~ to resign / feel ~ to respond

3 ~ and rob tourists / ~ someone's drink / ~ his victims

4 ~ as a global power / ~ from recession / the ideas ~ from ...

5 ~ the markets / ~ my nerves / ~ the angry crowd

6 ~ a wave of protests / ~ criticism / ~ fears

7 ~ the whole community / what ~ them is ... / ~ the (political) party

8 the country is ~ by recession / the trial has ~ the nation / ~ by fear

4 Work in groups. Make a list of reasons why people both tell urban myths and believe them. Then compare your list with another group. Which do you think is the most likely reason?

LISTENING

5 ▶ **2** Listen to three people telling urban myths. You won't hear the end of each story yet. Answer the questions about each story.

1 Who did it (supposedly) happen to?

2 Where did it happen?

3 Who else appears in the story?

4 What was the key thing that happened?

6 ▶ **2** Work in pairs. Retell the stories in as much detail as you can using these words. Then listen again and check your ideas.

1 stolen – reported – driveway – note – ill – concert – fantastic time

2 collapsed – rushed – diagnosed – poisoned – incident – the case

3 elderly – desperately sad – a loaf – freaked out – run out of – cashier – trolley – the spitting image – favour – good deed

7 ▶ **3** With your partner, discuss how you think each story will end. Then listen and see if you guessed correctly.

8 Work in groups. Discuss the questions.

• Which story do you like best? Why?

• What do you think of the main characters in the three stories? Why?

• What do you think the moral message of each story is?

• Do you agree with the messages?

UNDERSTANDING VOCABULARY

Binomials

Binomials are pairs of words usually linked together by *and*. The words are always used in the same order. The two main words in a binomial may: start with the same letter or contain similar sounds; be near synonyms; be connected in meaning or be opposites.

*He went to a supermarket to buy a few **bits and pieces**.*

*He was walking **up and down** the aisles.*

9 Complete the binomials in the sentences with these words.

foremost	miss	order	regulations	there
hard	off	quiet	then	tired

1 I've been studying Russian for about six years now **on and** _____.

2 There's a huge number of places to eat in the city, but the quality is a bit **hit and** _____.

3 I still like to party **every now and** _____, but I've calmed down a lot.

4 It's quite hard to find **peace and** _____ in the city.

5 I **thought long and** _____ about it before deciding.

6 It's a fairly affluent area, but there are still little pockets of poverty **here and** _____.

7 I can't take it anymore. I'm **sick and** _____ **of** the constant noise.

8 After the hurricane struck, there was a complete breakdown of **law and** _____ in the city.

9 The city's being ruined by the ever-growing number of stupid **rules and** _____.

10 Cities should be **first and** _____ places for kids.

10 Work in groups. Think of examples of the following:

1 three places where people who live in cities can go to get a bit of peace and quiet

2 three big decisions people usually have to think long and hard about

3 three things people that live in cities may get sick and tired of

4 two reasons why law and order might break down

5 two examples of stupid rules and regulations

SPEAKING

11 Work in pairs. Choose one of these tasks.

a Student A: read the urban myth in File 5 on page 97.

Student B: read the urban myth in File 6 on page 95.

Try to remember the details. Then tell your partner your story.

b Search the Internet for an urban myth that you find interesting and want to share with other students. Try to remember the details. Then tell your partner your story.

2

DUCKIE
YOUNG
SMITH

(VIRGIL)
TAMPA

HER HAIR IS
AS GRAY AS
HER HEART

A husband and wife who met at high school attend their school reunion

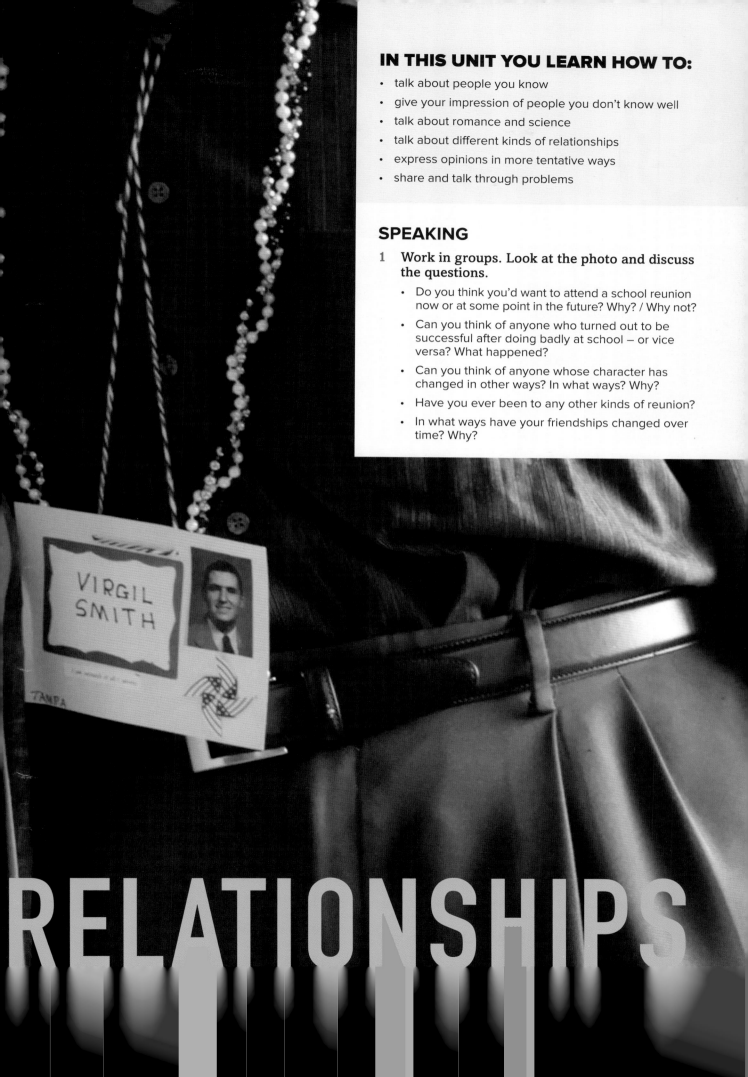

IN THIS UNIT YOU LEARN HOW TO:

- talk about people you know
- give your impression of people you don't know well
- talk about romance and science
- talk about different kinds of relationships
- express opinions in more tentative ways
- share and talk through problems

SPEAKING

1 **Work in groups. Look at the photo and discuss the questions.**

- Do you think you'd want to attend a school reunion now or at some point in the future? Why? / Why not?
- Can you think of anyone who turned out to be successful after doing badly at school – or vice versa? What happened?
- Can you think of anyone whose character has changed in other ways? In what ways? Why?
- Have you ever been to any other kinds of reunion?
- In what ways have your friendships changed over time? Why?

RELATIONSHIPS

GET THE IMPRESSION

VOCABULARY Describing people

1 **Choose the correct option.**

1 He's a complete *snobbish* / *snob*. He only talks to people who went to the 'right' school.

2 He's so *cynical* / *cynic*. He thinks everyone's got an agenda.

3 She has strong *principled* / *principles*. I completely trust her.

4 He's ever so *charming* / *charm*. He makes everyone feel special.

5 She's *a real* / *really* bitchy. She can be quite nasty about people.

6 She's a bit of *painful* / *a pain*. She really makes life difficult.

7 It's his sheer *arrogant* / *arrogance* that I hate. He thinks he knows it all.

8 She's completely *incompetent* / *incompetence*. She's really messed things up.

9 He's got a real *stubborn* / *stubbornness* streak. You won't get him to change his mind.

10 She's incredibly *intense* / *intensity*. We always seem to end up having quite heavy conversations.

11 She's very *willing* / *wilful* to listen. I'm sure you'll get a good response if you tell her what the problem is.

12 He's a right *laid-back* / *slacker*. He just seems to lie around all day.

2 **Work in pairs. Think of typical things the people in Exercise 1 might say.**

a snob: I couldn't possibly stay in a cheap hotel like that.

3 **Complete the sentences below with these pairs of words. Underline the whole phrase each word forms part of. The first one is done for you.**

back + undermine	~~mind + back down~~
bothered + notice	panics + stride
easiest + lighten up	remind + prone
boss + get ahead	shy + centre
exaggerating + seriously	stands up for + principles

1 Once he's <u>made up his *mind*</u>, he <u>won't *back down*</u> even if he's in the wrong.

2 She's constantly going behind my _____ and saying things to _____ me.

3 He never seems that _____ by criticism or bitchy comments. He just takes no _____ of it all.

4 She _____ what she believes in and she sticks to her _____. She's not easily bullied.

5 He's one of those people who never _____. He just takes everything in his _____.

6 She's not exactly _____ and retiring. She loves to be the _____ of attention.

7 He's not the _____ person to talk to. I wish he'd _____ a little.

8 You'll need to _____ her about it. She is _____ to forgetting things like that.

9 He's a bit prone to _____, so I wouldn't take what he said too _____.

10 She's the kind of person who's constantly sucking up to the _____ in order to _____.

4 **Work in pairs. Think of adjectives or nouns you could use to describe each of the people in Exercise 3.**

5   Work in pairs, Student A and B. Student A: say the sentences in Exercise 3. Student B: close your books. Respond to Student A using the adjectives you thought of in Exercise 4.

A: *Once he's made up his mind, he won't back down even if he's in the wrong.*

B: *I know, he's so stubborn. It drives me crazy sometimes!*

DEVELOPING CONVERSATIONS

Giving your impression

If we want to give our impression of people in the public eye or people we haven't met many times, we often use these structures.

He seems *fairly laid-back.*

She strikes me as *someone you can trust.*

He comes across as *a real gentleman.*

I get the impression / feeling *she's very principled.*

6   Work in pairs. Together, think of five people currently in the public eye. Then spend a few minutes thinking about your individual impressions of them and why you feel like this.

7   Share your impressions of each person using the structures in the box. Use the questions below in your conversation.

So what do you think of ...?

What do you make of ...?

What's your impression of ...?

LISTENING

8   ▶ 4 Listen to three conversations about different people. Answer the questions for each conversation.

1   Who is the person they mainly talk about?

2   What is the person like?

9   ▶ 4 Work in pairs. Try to remember the missing words from the sentences. Then listen again and check your answers.

1   a   He's _____ with him.

b   He always just gets really defensive and _____ big barrier.

c   Maybe you need to _____ and talk to his line manager about it?

2   a   I've always thought he _____ a really decent guy.

b   I just think you've got him wrong. He's _____ of various different causes.

3   a   She's really nice and very bright and chatty. We _____.

b   The only problem is she kind of _____ every morning.

c   The guy on the other side seems pleasant enough, but he _____ a bit of a slacker.

10   Work in groups. Discuss the questions.

•   What would you do in the first speaker's situation?

•   Do you know anyone who has a difficult relationship with their boss? Why?

•   Can you think of any celebrities who try to raise awareness of a cause? What's the cause? What do you think about it?

•   How common is it for people to share accommodation in your country?

•   Have you ever shared accommodation with anyone? If yes, how was it? If not, how would you feel about it?

•   Have you ever hit it off with someone straight away? Who with?

CONVERSATION PRACTICE

11   Write a name for each of the five kinds of people below. Think about: the words and phrases from this lesson you could use to describe them; examples of their behaviour or habits; the kinds of things they say or do; how you feel about them and why.

Someone:

1   in your family

2   that can be described with one or more words from Exercise 1

3   you get on really well with

4   quite unusual, eccentric or annoying

5   you admire

12   Work in pairs. Swap names. Ask and tell each other about the people on the lists. Find out as much as you can.

🎥 **2 To watch the video and do the activities, see the DVD ROM.**

GETTING TOGETHER

SPEAKING

1 **Work in groups. Discuss the questions.**

- What do you think are the pros and cons of the following ways of meeting a partner?
  - having an arranged marriage
  - going on a blind date
  - meeting through work or university
  - meeting via an Internet dating site

- How do you think the photo relates to meeting a partner? What do you think of this method?

- Which other ways of meeting partners can you think of? What's good / bad about each one?

READING

2 **Read the article opposite about love and relationships. Answer the questions.**

1 How are the three strands of science – social science, neuroscience and computer science – possibly helping to improve relationships?

2 How convinced is the author that science will actually provide benefits in this field?

3 **Work in pairs. Discuss why the following were mentioned.**

1 doing your own thing	5 kids
2 changing partners	6 thousands of online profiles
3 patience and perseverance	7 collaborative filtering
4 artists, poets and playwrights	8 arranged marriage

4 **Complete the sentences with some of the phrases in bold from the article.**

1 We constantly update the website and have special offers to _____.

2 As a company, we _____ building long-term relationships with our clients.

3 The important thing is _____ past failures.

4 There is now _____ to support the idea of banning laptop use in the classroom.

5 No single test would _____ the product is safe for human consumption.

6 I'm speaking at a conference for _____ biometrics.

7 The discovery _____ the key to developing a cure for dementia.

8 *The Guardian* spoke to Tim Watson about his clash with the press and how he _____.

5 **Choose two of the topics below to talk about. Spend a few minutes preparing what you want to say about each one. Then work in groups and share your ideas.**

- why divorce rates are rising

- how to have a long and happy relationship

- the pros and cons of having kids

- what you should look for in a partner

UNDERSTANDING VOCABULARY

Phrasal verbs

A phrasal verb is a verb with one or two linked particles. These particles are words we use as prepositions or adverbs in other contexts. Often the meaning of a phrasal verb is not obviously connected to either the verb or the particle.

*We've always **got on** very well.* (= We've always liked each other and been friendly.)

*You're expected to **come up with** clear ideas about who you're looking for.* (= suggest or think of)

As with normal verbs, you need to notice the collocations that phrasal verbs are used with. Some phrasal verbs may also:

- form part of commonly used phrases.

- be usually used in the passive.

- have more than one meaning.

- require object pronouns (*me, you, he, she, it, us, them*) to be placed between the verb and the particle.

6 **Use these phrasal verbs from the article to complete each group of phrases below.**

sound out	sort out	narrow down
be subjected to	end up	move into

1 ~ a place to stay / ~ a visa / ~ our differences / ~ the dispute

2 ~ a thorough examination / ~ terrible verbal abuse / ~ torture / ~ regular safety checks

3 ~ new premises / ~ publishing / ~ the Latin American market / ~ my new apartment

4 ~ voters / ~ your views / ~ the members of the board / ~ staff about the changes

5 ~ the list of suspects / ~ your options / ~ the focus of the essay / ~ your topic

6 ~ in trouble / ~ homeless / ~ getting to bed at four in the morning / ~ spending over £200

FROM CUPID TO COMPUTER

Rose McLoughlin explores the brave new relationship between romance and science

Fred and Doreen Wilson are not your average husband and wife. In fact, having just **celebrated their 75th wedding anniversary**, they may well enjoy the nation's longest-lasting marriage. 'There's no great secret to our success,' muses Fred. 'We've always got on very well and we've always respected each other, but neither of us has ever expected the other to be the only source of happiness in life. We've been off and done our own things, but we've always come back to each other afterwards and that's helped **keep things fresh**. When things go badly, people often think changing partners will help, but hardly anyone ever ends up better off as a result.'

Given that in many European countries over six out of ten **marriages** now **end in divorce** and even in more culturally conservative places rates of 20% are no longer uncommon, such patience and perseverance may seem like **a thing of the past**. In fact, though, researchers are convinced that we can all learn how to be happier by **drawing lessons from** couples like the Wilsons.

Over recent years, social science has increasingly moved into what was traditionally the domain of artists, poets and playwrights, and one result has been **a wealth of studies** exploring love and marriage and the experiences of those who've been through it all already – and **lived to tell the tale**. This research reveals that we have more chance of staying together if we **contribute equally to** the household, don't attempt to sort out problems by text message, get plenty of sleep … and avoid having kids!

While social scientists analyse the wisdom of life-long partners, **researchers working in the field of** neuroscience believe they can now **detect the signs of** true romance in those embarking on new relationships by observing which parts of their brain light up – and to what degree they do so – during scans. Distinctive patterns of electrical activity are noticeable in volunteers who claim to have recently fallen in love and an informed viewing of neuron activity could **be sufficient to determine whether** their feelings are strong enough for their relationships to last.

However, it is in the field of online dating that the appliance of science **may well prove to be** most lucrative. Where early sites simply promised access to thousands upon thousands of profiles, an excess of choice that did not result in **a huge increase in the number of** couples finding love, their modern counterparts are increasingly narrowing down our choices by using sophisticated mathematical formulas to try to ensure subscribers are matched to those they are supposedly most compatible with.

Subscribe to a site today and you're expected to not only come up with clear ideas about who you're looking for but to also answer upwards of 200 extra questions designed to sound out your morals, values and beliefs. These details are then subjected to an analysis called collaborative filtering, whereby the preferences of large numbers of people are collected and divided into groups of similar users.

There is, of course, a deep irony in all of this. In the West, we tend to regard arranged marriage as an outdated relic from a distant era and we **pride ourselves on** our freedom and individuality. Yet it could easily be claimed that we've simply replaced one kind of (human) matchmaker with another technological one. **The degree to which this will** ensure marital success **remains highly contested**. Perhaps, in the end, we may have to accept that chemistry will never be completely understood by scientists!

---

7 Look at these phrases containing two-word phrasal verbs which have already featured in this book. Which phrasal verbs usually use object pronouns between the verb and the particle? Which have the pronoun after the particle?

1 bring in new restrictions
2 drag down the rest of the team
3 embark on a strategy
4 give away his millions
5 go through huge changes
6 knock down the slums
7 set out an ambitious plan
8 set up a recycling centre
9 stick to your principles
10 take over the bathroom

8 ▶ **5** Listen and check your answers.

9 Work in groups. Answer the questions.

1 How important do you think it is to stick to your principles? Can you think of times when maybe it's better to abandon them?

2 Do you know anyone who's ever quit their job and embarked on a whole new career?

3 Which people you know have been through the biggest changes since you've known them?

4 Can you remember a time you ended up spending more money than you'd planned to?

5 Do you know anyone who's ever set up a company?

MIXED MESSAGES

Chicago Sky coach Pokey Chatman talks with students during a charity event

SPEAKING

1 Choose which relationships from the box below you have had. Put them in order from the biggest influence on your life to the smallest influence. Then work in groups. Compare and explain your choices.

siblings	grandparent – grandchild
life partners	parent – child
colleagues	teacher – pupil
business partners	coach – athlete
neighbours	doctor – patient

LISTENING

2 ▶ 6 Listen to five people talking about a young man called Toby and an incident he's been involved in. Decide:

1 who each speaker is and what their relationship to Toby is.

2 what you think the incident they refer to was.

3 ▶ 6 Work in pairs. Check you understand the phrases in bold, then discuss the questions. Listen again and check your ideas.

1 What were the **mixed messages** Toby received?

2 What will help him **get back on the straight and narrow**, according to his grandmother?

3 How did the **ridiculous confrontation** come about?

4 Why do you think Toby was **unwilling to back down**?

5 Why has the incident **come as a shock** to his coach?

6 What did Toby **confide to** his coach?

7 Why did the doctor say the man **was in remarkably good health**?

8 Who **came to his aid**?

9 Why did they split up, **when it came down to it**?

10 Where was there **a scene** and what do you think caused it?

GRAMMAR

Would

Would has many different uses, including talking about past habits, giving advice, talking about the future in the past, and explaining hypothetical consequences in conditional sentences.

completed Ch.

4 Match each sentence from the listening (1–6) to a sentence (a–f) that has the same meaning of *would*.

1 I probably would've stayed with him if he'd apologised.
2 When he was a toddler, I'd do the childcare most days.
3 I knew it would come to no good, but you can't really interfere, can you?
4 I remember once I asked him to change desks and he just wouldn't – just refused point blank.
5 He should obviously be punished, but after that I'd still give him another chance.
6 I would say he has a stubborn streak and he's been prone to outbursts and answering back.

a I'd consider talking it through with a therapist. You shouldn't bottle these things up.
b For some reason, the car wouldn't start this morning so I'm waiting for the breakdown people.
c They said it would be miserable today, but it's actually turned out quite nice.
d If they'd intervened, the situation would be a lot worse now.
e Before the anger management classes, he'd often get into unnecessary confrontations.
f I wouldn't say it's a disaster – just a slight setback.

 Check your ideas on page 87 and do Exercise 1.

5 Use structures and phrases with *would* to write sentences about the story of Toby. Think about:

- what you'd say his childhood was like – what he and his parents would do and how they got on.
- why you'd say different people have the opinions they do.
- why you think he was arrested and how it would've been different in other circumstances.
- what you'd imagine / hope would happen to Toby now.
- what you would advise him and the people he knows to do.

I'd say he had a difficult childhood because his parents would argue a lot and they wouldn't spend a lot of time with him.

I would've thought Toby still likes his ex-girlfriend.

6 Work in groups. Share your ideas and see if you agree.

G For further practice, see Exercise 2 on page 88.

VOCABULARY Relationships

7 Work in pairs. For each sentence below, decide:

a what relationship in Exercise 1 you think is being talked about.
b if you think the relationship is good or bad – and why.
c if you could say this about any relationships you know.

1 They're **going through a bit of a rough patch** and have talked about splitting up.
2 I **keep an eye on her** as she's quite frail and has no relatives nearby.

3 As a teenager, she really **sparked my interest in** science.
4 I've **collaborated with him on** a number of projects and he's taught me a lot.
5 They're **not on speaking terms** at the moment, which can **make it awkward** at meetings.
6 We're **on first-name terms** as I have to go and see him so often.
7 They **maintain a professional relationship**, but they **don't see eye to eye** on many issues.
8 They **get on each other's nerves** all the time and they're constantly **competing for** my **attention**.
9 She **puts people at their ease** and reassures them about the whole process.
10 He **pushes his kids incredibly hard**.
11 I don't really know any of them as we tend to **keep ourselves to ourselves**.
12 He **doesn't** tend to **pull his weight**, which causes some **friction** in the office.

SPEAKING

8 Work in groups of three. You are going to roleplay some conversations.

Student A: look at File 7 on page 97.

Student B: look at File 8 on page 95.

Student C: look at File 9 on page 96.

Read your three problems and choose the one that you think is most interesting. Plan how to describe the problem as if it was really happening to you. Think about some details to add.

9 Now roleplay a conversation about each problem. You can start the conversations like this:

A: *What's up?*
B: *Oh, it's …* (explain the problem)

Continue the conversations by sympathising, sharing experiences, giving advice, offering reassurance, etc. Use some of the language below.

- Oh dear!
- That must be difficult.
- How awful!
- I know exactly what you're going through!
- Something similar happened to a friend of mine.
- I'd talk it over with them (if I were you).
- Have you been in touch with the police?
- I'd have thought they could help.
- I'd imagine it'll all blow over.
- I wouldn't worry about it.
- What an idiot!

10 When you have discussed one problem each, choose another one or invent your own relationship issue. Have further conversations.

VIDEO 1

BIG CITY CONSTRUCTION

1 Work in pairs. Check you understand the phrases below. Discuss what you think could go wrong with each of these aspects of building a skyscraper, what the consequences of the errors might be, and how they might be resolved.

- get planning permission
- employ a building crew
- blast a hole for the foundations
- bring in and remove materials from the site
- erect and operate cranes
- deal with suppliers
- ensure site safety
- protect adjacent buildings

2 Work in groups. Rank the topics in Exercise 1 in order of how difficult you think they will be when developing a site like the one in the photo (1= the most difficult, 8= the least difficult).

3 ▶ 3 Watch the video and decide what you think the three main challenges are. How do they resolve them?

4 ▶ 3 Work in pairs. Do you remember any of the numbers missing from the sentences? Watch again and complete the sentences.

1 There are nearly _____ skyscrapers in New York City.

2 When preparing the foundations, it took a year to remove _____ cubic metres of earth.

3 About _____ pounds of building material comes in on each truck every day and they do around _____ lifts each day.

4 The building crew are working about _____ metres above ground level.

5 The average weight of a load of steel beams is about _____ tons.

6 The trucks sometimes have to cut across _____ lanes in order to turn.

7 The five water tanks will eventually contain _____ litres of water.

8 The spire is assembled from _____ pieces at a height of _____ metres above ground.

9 Once complete, the building will stand at _____ metres high.

5 Work in groups. Discuss the questions.

- What do you think of the building design in the video? What do you think the building is for?
- What buildings that you know would you describe with each of the adjectives below? Why?
  amazing   hideous   unusual   controversial
- What buildings are being erected in your town at the moment?
- What are they for? Do you think they're a good idea? Why? / Why not?
- Have you ever had to put up with building work? Where? What happened?

UNDERSTANDING FAST SPEECH

6 ▶ 4 Listen to an extract from the video said at natural pace. Try to write down what you hear. Then compare your ideas with a partner.

7 ▶ 5 Try again. This time you will hear a slower version of the extract.

8 Check your ideas in File 10 on page 98. Groups of words are marked with / and pauses are marked //. Stressed sounds are in CAPITALS. Practise saying the extract.

REVIEW 1

VOCABULARY

1 Complete the text with one word in each space.

Many people ¹_____ now consider New York to be among the safest major cities in the world, but it has ²_____ to overcome huge problems to reach this situation. Back in 1990, the place was ³_____ a war zone, with the murder rate ⁴_____ risen to almost 2,500 a year and thousands of shootings taking place too. Fewer and ⁵_____ tourists ⁶_____ venture beyond a small central area of the city. So how did New York manage to restore law and ⁷_____ and become what it is today? First and ⁸_____, its citizens got to the point where they were ⁹_____ and tired of the situation and demanded political change. The government brought ¹⁰_____ tougher and more efficient policing. However, this probably would not ¹¹_____ been enough on its own without an economic recovery and huge investment in the poorest areas of the city. Successive governments stuck ¹²_____ these policies to ensure success.

2 Complete the second sentence so that it has a similar meaning to the first sentence using the word given. Do not change the word given. You must use between three and five words, including the word given.

1 We generally used to play in the street when we were kids.
By _____ in the street when were kids. **WOULD**

2 If you ask me, he's too demanding of the kids.
I would _____ the kids too hard. **SAID**

3 The city is completely different to what it was like when I lived there.
The city _____ some huge changes since I lived here. **THROUGH**

4 I know the coach was bad, but it's terrible that people abused him that way.
The coach should _____ abuse like that, however bad he was. **SUBJECTED**

5 From what I heard, they have reduced the list of candidates to five.
They seem _____ list to five candidates. **NARROWED**

6 Things still need to improve, but at least they demolished the slums.
The city would be a lot worse if they _____ the slums. **DOWN**

3 Choose the correct option.

1 I doubt you will *hear / have heard* of the place I come from.

2 We got approval for a loan to start a restaurant so we're hoping to *set it up / set up it* next year.

3 The mayor introduced sweeping changes *being elected / having been elected* by a huge majority.

4 I wish we *would do / had done* something about the litter before it got so bad.

5 I knew the whole venture *would fail / will fail* as soon as we *embarked on it / embarked it on*.

VOCABULARY

4 Match the verbs (1–8) with the collocates (a–h).

1	undergo	a	me / my authority
2	demolish	b	huge changes / an operation
3	undermine	c	the decline / traffic
4	set out	d	restrictions / a heavy fine
5	impose	e	on the fumes / on a bone
6	spark	f	a building / all his arguments
7	choke	g	my interest / waves of protest
8	halt	h	an ambitious plan / the options

5 What do the adjectives describe? Put them into two groups.

condemned	vibrant	stubborn	sprawling
prone	principled	congested	laid-back
willing	affluent		

6 Complete the idioms with a preposition in each space. Then think of a real example for each one.

1 She takes everything _____ her stride.

2 They don't see eye _____ eye on many issues.

3 He often goes _____ my back.

4 We're not _____ speaking terms.

5 He has to be the centre _____ attention.

6 There's a real buzz _____ the place.

7 She really puts people _____ their ease.

8 It really gets _____ my nerves.

7 Complete the sentences. Use the word in brackets to form a word that fits in the space.

1 He can be very _____ about food. Only the most expensive will do. (snob)

2 I think you need a bit of _____ to be successful. (arrogant)

3 We stayed in this _____ little village. (charm)

4 People are quite _____ about politicians, but I think we can change things. (cynic)

5 The city became run-down because of the sheer _____ of city council. (competent)

6 It's quite a rough area. I've heard about several _____ round there. (mug)

7 He can be very aggressive and he gets involved in stupid _____ about nothing. (confront)

8 The doctor said I was in _____ good health. (remark)

8 Complete the text with one word in each space. The first letters are given.

I shared a flat with a friend at university, Miguel. We were fine most of the time but ¹n_____ and again we'd ²e_____ u_____ having an argument. Cleaning caused the most ³fr_____. Miguel is quite intense and fussy. He can't stand seeing even a ⁴tr_____ of dirt in the house, whereas I'm a bit more ⁵l_____-b_____. He'd sometimes accuse me of not pulling my ⁶we_____, which would annoy me because I often cooked for him, so I'd tell him to ⁷li_____ u_____ and that the place didn't have to be absolutely ⁸sp_____ all the time.

completed for chabata.

3

CULTURE AND IDENTITY

The centuries-old village tradition of *galena*, Ribnovo

IN THIS UNIT YOU LEARN HOW TO:

- discuss different aspects of culture and society
- politely disagree with people's opinions
- express feelings and opinions more emphatically
- describe useful objects and household jobs
- discuss your own personal and national identities

SPEAKING

1 **Work in pairs. Look at the photo and discuss the questions.**

- Who do you think the people are?
- In what country do you think the photo was taken?
- What do you think is happening in the photo?
- What do you think it might say about the culture of the place and people?
- How important do you think it is to maintain traditions? Why?

VOCABULARY Society and culture

2 **Check you understand the words and phrases in bold. Then discuss to what degree the sentences apply to your country.**

1 The people are incredibly welcoming because **hospitality** is central to the culture.

2 It's quite **male-dominated**. Women are looked down on and there's still a lot of discrimination.

3 It's quite conservative, so if you don't **conform**, life can be quite difficult.

4 Religion **plays a powerful role** in society.

5 Everything's very **bureaucratic**. You need a permit or ID card for everything.

6 I think it's a very family-centred culture. Most people's social life **revolves around** their extended family.

7 It's basically a very **secular society** and people have **lost touch with** their traditions.

8 Socially, it's a very liberal society. People don't like to **interfere** – it's very much **live and let live**.

9 Life is **tough**, but people generally have a very **positive outlook**.

10 **Class** is a big thing. People are very aware of your background and there's not much **social mobility**.

11 Humour is a key part of how people **relate to** each other. People often **take the mickey** out of each other.

12 People are very **reserved** – you can only relate to them **on a superficial level**.

3 **Do you think the descriptions in Exercise 2 are good for a country? Why? / Why not? In each case, try to think of one flip side.**

THINGS ARE DIFFERENT THERE

DEVELOPING CONVERSATIONS

Challenging overgeneralisations

When people use stereotypes or overgeneralise, we often want to challenge what they say – or moderate it. We can use various phrases to do this.

Come on!

That's a bit harsh / of an overstatement / a stereotype, **isn't it?!**

I wouldn't go that far.

What? Everyone? / **All** women?

It's not as though we're all like that.

That can't be true! It's like saying all Dutch people are tall!

Just because you're Brazilian, it **doesn't mean** you like football.

There must be loads of British people who don't drink tea!

1 **Work in pairs. Take turns to say and respond to the overgeneralisations below. Use the phrases in the box.**

1 Men are no good at listening.

2 Women are terrible drivers.

3 Young people these days have no respect.

4 The people from the South are more friendly.

5 The rich are only interested in themselves.

6 People who are on benefits are just lazy – they don't want to work.

7 The British are such hypocrites!

8 How come you speak my language? You're British!

2 **Work in groups. Discuss the questions.**

- What stereotypes are there of your country?
- Are there stereotypes of people from particular cities or areas in your country?
- Are any of these stereotypes positive? How fair do you think they are?
- Do you think you've ever been stereotyped? How?

LISTENING

3 ▶ **7** Listen to three conversations about society and culture in different countries. Answer the questions for each conversation.

   1 What aspect/s of culture do they talk about?

   2 Are the speakers talking about their own culture?

   3 What feelings are expressed about the culture?

4 ▶ **7** Are the sentences true (T), false (F) or not mentioned (N)? Listen again and check your answers.

   1 a Zoe's partner is from a different country.

      b The people Mehdi works with are making fun of him.

      c Mehdi wants to change jobs.

   2 a They don't have enough admin people.

      b People are happy to queue.

   3 a The speaker stayed with friends who live there.

      b Most women don't work.

      c The government is encouraging changes in attitudes to women.

5 **Work in groups. Discuss the questions.**

- Do you know any couples who are from different cultures? Where are they from?
- Do you think different countries have a different sense of humour? Why? In what way?
- Have you ever misinterpreted something or been misinterpreted? What happened?
- What is your best / worst experience of bureaucracy?
- Do you think the government can change aspects of culture?
- What effect can each of the following have on society and culture?
  TV & film education money travel & immigration

GRAMMAR

Cleft sentences

The sentences below, based on the listening, use the common structure of subject–verb–object:

He seems to be struggling with the people.

He hates all the bitchy comments and gossip.

They only stared at their computer screens or filed papers.

They only ever seem to have one person serving you. It really frustrates me.

However, we sometimes use different sentence structures to highlight particular aspects – the subject or object, the feelings people have, the actions people do, etc.

6 **Work in pairs. Look at audio script 7 on page 103 to see the actual sentences that the examples in the box are based on. Answer the questions.**

   1 How does the sentence structure change?

   2 What words / phrases begin the sentence?

   3 What extra words (if any) are added to the sentence?

   4 Why did the speaker want to add this emphasis?

G Check your ideas on page 88 and do Exercise 1.

P168

7 **Complete the dialogue by making cleft sentences using the words in italics. You will need to add words and you may need to change the form of the verbs.**

A: I think it's a shame we don't keep up traditions here anymore.

B: Yeah, but [1]*thing / like about our way of life / fact / be yourself.*

A: Yeah, but [2]*what / concern / people lose touch with their roots.*

B: Come on. It's not as though we've become a classless society. In fact, [3]*one / frustrate / lack / social mobility.*

A: Maybe – but the government could do something about that.

B: [4]*it / not the government / do something; / people's attitudes / need to change.*

A: I wouldn't go that far. I'm not sure it's that bad.

B: Well, I guess. [5]*one / give / hope / fact / young people / don't seem all that interested in people's backgrounds.*

A: Only because they aren't interested in anything! [6]*all / want / go shopping.*

B: That's a bit harsh. There are loads of young people who take an interest in politics.

8 **Work in pairs. Practise reading out the dialogue.**

9 **Complete the sentences so they are true for you. Use the ideas in brackets.**

   1 The thing I find most _____ about my _____ (person) is _____.

   2 The main thing I *love / hate* about my _____ (person) is _____.

   3 All I tend to do most _____ (day / time) is _____ and _____.

   4 The place I'd most like to visit is _____.

   5 One _____ I have absolutely no interest in *visiting / trying* is _____.

   6 The main reason that I _____ (activity) is _____.

10 **Work in pairs. Compare your sentences and explain your ideas.**

G For further practice, see Exercises 2 and 3 on page 89.

CONVERSATION PRACTICE

11 **You are going to have a conversation about the place where you live now. Make a list of things that you like about the place and another list of things that annoy you.**

12 **Work in groups. Explain your ideas. Agree or disagree with your partners. Use as much language from this lesson as you can.**

▶ 6 To watch the video and do the activities, see the DVD ROM.

IT'S A CULTURAL THING

SPEAKING

1 **Work in groups. Discuss the questions.**
   - Do you think the place you live in is typical of homes in your country? Why? / Why not?
   - Think of the objects in your house. Which do you think are very common in homes in your country? Do you have any objects that are less typical? Why?
   - Have you ever been in any homes in other countries? If yes, was there anything about them that you thought was strange or unusual?
   - In what ways do you think homes / rooms / household objects can reflect a person's nationality or personal cultural identity?

VOCABULARY Household objects

2 **Match the actions on the left with the objects on the right they usually go with. More than one verb may be possible with some objects.**

climb	load
cover	run
cut	spread
fill	stick in
flush	thread
heat	unblock
lay	wring out

bucket	oven
carpet	pan
cloth	pin
dishwasher	sink
glue	string
ladder	tap
needle	toilet

3 **Work in pairs. Discuss the difference between the following:**

rope and string   a mop and a brush

wire and cable   a nail and a screw

a cloth and a sponge   a ladder and stairs

a bucket and a bowl   a knee pad and a bandage

a drill and a hammer   soap and washing-up liquid

4 **Decide which five actions below are problems. Discuss with your partner what would need to be done after each of them. Which five are solutions? To what kind of problems?**

spill some water	flood the kitchen
rip your trousers	sweep the floor
soak your jeans	drop a glass
stain your top	rinse a glass
mend your shirt	wipe the table

5 **With your partner, take turns to choose objects or actions from Exercises 2, 3 and 4. Either draw, act or explain them without using the actual words on this page. Your partner should say the name of the object / action.**

READING

6 **Read the introduction to an article about differences people noticed when living in other countries. Decide which sentence below best summarises the point the writer is making.**

1 The way we feel when we're abroad is similar to how foreigners feel in our countries.

2 It can be really shocking to discover how different homes in other countries are.

3 Definitions of normality vary across time and across different countries.

4 Globalisation means more people around the world have the same kinds of things in their homes.

5 Travel helps to broaden our minds and shows how we're similar to – and different from – others.

7 **Work in pairs. Discuss the questions.**
   - How far do you agree with the basic point of the introduction?
   - Can you think of anything that:
     - you sometimes take for granted?
     - you've reacted to with confusion or disgust?
     - your culture has adopted from abroad?

8 **Read the rest of the article. Then discuss the questions with your partner.**
   - Are any of the things mentioned usual in homes in your country?
   - Would you like to have any of the things mentioned in your house? If so, why?
   - Which of the things mentioned do you find the strangest? Why?
   - Did any of the things mentioned help you understand these countries better?

9 **Read the article again. Match each of the following to the people in the article.**
   Which person:

1 gets a puzzled reaction when they explain where they lived before?

2 initially felt slightly restricted in the kitchen?

3 is deprived of a luxury they used to enjoy?

4 has adapted to cold winds blowing into rooms?

5 mentions an object that helps people relax together?

6 was surprised how well people cope without a particular object?

7 found the space where a common household chore gets done a bit odd?

8 expresses considerable frustration?

10 **Think about your own answers to the questions below. Then work in groups and compare your ideas.**
   - Which household objects do you think most reflect your national culture? In what way?
   - Can you think of three objects that you strongly associate with other countries?
   - Which household objects would you find it hardest to live without? Why?

FOREIGN OBJECTS

In our globalised world, we often take it for granted that the things that surround us are universal, sensible and normal. So when we travel or live abroad and discover new objects – or the absence of ones we expected to find – it can be surprising. We may react with confusion or disgust, but it's always good to bear in mind the fact that visitors travelling to our own countries must doubtless have similar experiences. It's also worth remembering that what we see as extraordinary or ridiculous today, we may end up adopting as our own in the future. Take an English aristocrat's comment on seeing a bizarre instrument in 17th century Italy: 'Why should a person need a fork when God had given him hands?'

IN-HA, SOUTH KOREA

I've more or less got used to most of the odd things I've encountered in Britain – the houses that are old and draughty; the fitted carpets on the stairs and even in the bathrooms; the presence of kettles and toasters in every single kitchen. One thing I still struggle to understand, though, is why so many places still have separate hot and cold taps at the sink rather than a mixer tap. You have to fill the sink in order to get the water at the right temperature, but then you can't rinse your face properly because the soap stays in the water. It's much better with a mixer tap because you can wash with running water. In fact, what drives you really mad is if there's no plug. Then you end up either getting freezing hands or burning them – or trying to move between the two. Useless!

JIM, NORTHERN IRELAND

There are loads of things I've noticed here in Spain that are different to back home. For example, in Belfast I used to live in a basement flat, which people here find really weird as basements are mainly used for storing things! Then there's all the kitchen equipment: we've got a *jamonero*, which is a kind of clamp that holds meat in place while you slice it; and a *paellera*, which is this flat, round, shallow pan with two handles for cooking paella in. A lot of the time, folk cook on gas burners to ensure the heat is evenly distributed, so of course we have one of those as well. Best of all, though, is the *brasero* – a kind of electric heater that you place under a table covered with a long cloth going right down to the floor. All the heat gets kept in and it's lovely and cosy when everyone's sitting round the table.

KASIA, POLAND

I'm Polish, my husband is Brazilian and we met in Sweden! We've been living in his hometown of Belo Horizonte for the last four years now and life is different here. For example, back in Lublin, I used to love soaking in a nice hot bath, but here we don't even have a tub! It's much more of a shower culture here – usually both before and after work as it's so hot and humid. Another weird thing for me is the fact that the place we're renting has a large, deep separate sink next to the washing machine in this kind of little utility area, where your clothes can be soaked and scrubbed and more delicate items can be washed. Oh, and I mustn't forget that staple of Brazilian kitchens: the pressure cooker. We use ours all the time, especially when cooking black beans – *feijão*.

ED, CANADA

I spent two years living and working in Qingdao, on the east coast of China, and found the homes there quite fascinating. Most people I knew there live in apartments in high-rise blocks and though they do have some modern appliances, dryers were unusual and you'd often see washing hung out to dry on the balconies. Some places lack fridges too, which didn't seem to bother people as much as you'd expect as all the food is bought fresh in the market every day. My place didn't have an oven either, which somewhat reduced the scope of my cooking, though I got pretty good at using a wok – a big, round Chinese frying pan – on just a single gas ring. One other weird thing I remember is that when you enter a Chinese home, you'll usually find a shoe shelf that you place your shoes on while visiting.

A UNITED KINGDOM?

SPEAKING

1   Work in groups. Discuss the questions.

- Look at the photos. What aspects of UK culture do you think each one shows?

- How do you think each of the things in the box below is connected to UK culture?

Bonfire Night	God Save the Queen
car boot sales	Islam
Carnival	the NHS
curry	the public school system
fish and chips	regional autonomy
football	St George's Day
Glastonbury	the trade union movement

- What else do you know about UK culture? Think about: literature, theatre, music, broadcasting, visual arts, fashion, religion, cuisine, sport, buildings, monuments.

- How important is UK culture in the world? In your country? For you personally?

LISTENING

2   ▶ 8 Listen to three people from the UK talking about their own cultural identities. Which three things from the box in Exercise 1 does each person mention and why?

3   ▶ 8 Listen again. Are the sentences true (T) or false (F)? How do you know?

1 a Savannah's parents were from different ethnic backgrounds.

   b The place she lives in is very racially diverse.

   c Her friends in the city often laugh at her.

2 a Callum gets annoyed by a common false assumption.

   b He complains about how tight government control of Scotland still is.

   c His outlook is fairly narrow and provincial.

3 a Amir acknowledges he doesn't conform to a certain stereotype.

   b He gets quite upset about the things people sometimes say to him.

   c He retains a sense of his family roots.

4   Work in pairs. Discuss the questions.

- What was the most interesting thing you heard? What was the most surprising? Why?

- How racially diverse is your country? How common is it to see mixed-race couples?

- Are there strong regional differences in your country?

- Do you think it's good for regions to have a lot of autonomy from central government?

UNDERSTANDING VOCABULARY

Words and phrases

In the listening, you heard the phrases *it's no big thing* and *a whole new thing*. Many words like *thing* are used as part of fixed phrases. These phrases sometimes have meanings that aren't obviously connected to the meaning of the single words in them. At Advanced level, it's not enough to just know single words. You need to learn as many phrases as you can.

5 Make phrases with *thing* by putting the words in brackets in the correct order.

1 Don't make such a fuss. _____. (really / is / thing / big / no / it)

2 It's rude. _____ (just / thing / the / is / not / done / it) in our society.

3 I'd love to do it, but _____ (fine / be / a / thing / chance / would)!

4 _____ (the / mind / is / from / it / my / thing / furthest) at the moment.

5 I always do it _____ (morning / in / the / thing / first).

6 _____ (makes / you / sort / it / that / the / thing / is / of) glad to be alive.

7 It's difficult, _____ (with / another / one / thing / what / and).

8 I didn't plan it. _____ (thing / to / one / another / led / just).

6 Work in pairs. Discuss what *it* could be in each of the sentences in Exercise 5.

7 ▶ 9 Listen to the phrases from Exercise 5 and notice which sounds are stressed. Then listen again and repeat the phrases.

8 Work in groups. In the listening in Exercise 2, you also heard the phrase *die laughing*. Think of five more phrases using either the word *die* or the word *laugh*. Write example sentences to show how they're used. Use a dictionary to help you if you need to.

LISTENING

9 ▶ 10 Listen to part of a lecture about identity. Summarise the main message in a sentence.

10 Work in pairs. Compare your ideas and discuss how far you agree with this message.

11 ▶ 10 Listen again. Why was each of the following mentioned?

1 global uncertainty

2 commerce

3 a French TV show and a German car

4 a ballet lover and a marketing manager

5 terrible tensions

6 the ruling elite

12 Work in pairs. Which sentences below do you think the lecturer would agree with? Explain your ideas by referring to things the lecturer said.

1 Globalisation has led to an increase in nationalism.

2 We should all buy more locally-made products in order to boost the economy.

3 You could easily have more in common with someone in a different country than with your neighbour.

4 Every single person living in a society contributes equally to the nation's identity.

5 Schools play a key role in developing critical thinking about culture and identity.

6 More and more people are going to suffer identity crises in the future.

SPEAKING

13 Work in groups. Choose one of these tasks. Then spend a few minutes preparing for the task on your own.

a Make a list of eight people or things from your country that you think are culturally important. Think about: people, cultural / youth movements, kinds of food / drink, special days, places, sports, etc.

b Make a list of eight people or things from anywhere in the world that are an important part of your own cultural identity. Think about: people, historical events, books, films, music, kinds of food / drink, places, sports and sporting events, etc.

14 Now take turns to present your lists to your group and to explain them. Your partners should comment or ask questions to find out more.

4

POLITICS

IN THIS UNIT YOU LEARN HOW TO:

- describe politicians and their qualities
- give opinions about politics
- talk about consequences of political proposals
- tell jokes
- talk about voting and elections

SPEAKING

1 **Work in pairs. Look at the photo and discuss the questions.**

- Do you know which country the parliament building in the photo is in?
- What do you think the building says about the way the country wants to portray itself?
- How similar / different is the parliament building in your country?
- Have you ever been to the parliament building in your country?

2 **Choose the five qualities below that you think politicians most need. Then explain your ideas to your partner.**

honesty	compassion
ruthlessness	flexibility
passion	bravery
charisma	excellent communication skills
self-confidence	the ability to compromise

The National Congress building designed by Oscar Niemeyer

I DON'T KNOW WHERE I STAND

DEVELOPING CONVERSATIONS
Giving opinions

1   Find six pairs of sentences with a similar meaning.

1   I'm a huge fan of the idea.   12
2   I don't really know where I stand.   5
3   I'm totally against it.   10
4   I think the negatives far outweigh the positives.   8
5   I can't pass judgement. I don't know enough about it.   (2)
6   It's a good idea in theory, just not in practice.   9
7   I am in favour. I just have some slight reservations.   11
8   I have some major doubts about it.
9   It's OK in principle. I just think it's unworkable.
10   I'm completely opposed to it.
11   It's not without problems, but on the whole I like it.
12   I'm totally in favour of it.

2   Work in groups. Use sentences from Exercise 1 to explain how you feel about the following:

- nuclear energy
- globalisation
- free health care
- putting up taxes
- increasing military spending
- raising the age of retirement to 70
- introducing a maximum wage
- your country hosting a major international event
- limiting the working week to a maximum of 35 hours
- banning cars from city centres

LISTENING

3   ▶ 11 Listen to two conversations about topics from Exercise 2. Answer the questions for each conversation.

1   What is the topic of the conversation?
2   Where does each person stand on the issue?

4   ▶ 11 Work in pairs. Look at these sentences from the conversations. Decide which are incorrect and then correct them. Listen again and check your answers.

Conversation 1

1   Some of these salaries are obscene.
2   It all just puts up prices.
3   They'd just detail it as part of their income.
4   They'd be able to find ways through it.
5   I'm just playing devil's advocate.

Conversation 2

6   Did you hear about this proposal to bid to hold the Olympics here?
7   Won't the Games earn a lot of money?
8   They always talk about them leaving a good facility.
9   We don't have a hope in hell.
10   It'd be a receipt for disaster.

5   With your partner, discuss the questions.

- Which of the opinions expressed do you have most / least sympathy with? Why?
- What are the advantages of playing devil's advocate? Are there any downsides?
- In what other ways might cities run up huge debts?
- Have you ever heard any stories about cities going bankrupt? Where? What happened?

GRAMMAR

Conditionals 1

Conditionals can be used to talk about general truths as well as both probable and imagined events now or in the future. They usually – but not always – introduce conditions with the word *if*.

6 Match 1–5 to a–e to make extracts from the conversations.

1 And what would you include in pay?
2 Even if they do manage to introduce this new law,
3 Imagine if we actually won it.
4 If they're earning that much,
5 As long as there's the official desire to make it work,

a it encourages other people to ask for more.
b It'd be a recipe for disaster.
c Supposing they were given a boat, or whatever, instead of money?
d then it'll work.
e it's basically going to be unworkable.

7 Work in pairs. Look at the extracts in Exercise 6 and answer the questions.

1 Which sentence describes something generally true?
2 Which sentences describe probable events in the future?
3 Which sentences describe imagined events now / in the future?
4 What tenses are used in the conditional parts of each sentence?
5 What structures are used in the result clauses?
6 Which other words apart from *if* are used to introduce conditions?

G Check your ideas on page 89 and do Exercise 1.

8 Work in pairs. Use different conditional structures to think of at least two responses to each sentence. Then compare your ideas with another pair. Who has the best ideas?

1 I'm not going to vote. What's the point? It's not like it makes any difference, does it?
2 They say they're going to make it much harder for people to get into the country.
3 I read somewhere that they're going to start privatising more of the health service.
4 He's been accused of lying about his expenses and claiming more than he should've done.
5 He can't go on holiday now, not with a crisis like this developing.
6 Smoking kills thousands every year. It should just be completely banned.

G For further practice, see Exercise 2 on page 90.

VOCABULARY Consequences

9 Complete the sentences with these verbs.

bankrupt	boost	devastate	lead
trigger	benefit	compound	discourage
reduce	undermine		

1 It might _____ people from working.
2 It might _____ the rich, but it'll harm the poor.
3 It'll _____ the economy and result in the creation of new jobs.
4 It could _____ the whole area and leave thousands unemployed.
5 It'd put an enormous strain on finances. It could _____ the city.
6 It's a bad idea. If anything, it'll _____ the existing social problems.
7 It might _____ an election earlier than they wanted.
8 It's bad. It'll _____ relations between the two countries.
9 It might help to _____ drug abuse.
10 It'll create divisions and _____ to tension.

10 Work in pairs. Think of one event that could make each of the things in Exercise 9 happen.

If they put up taxes, it might discourage people from working.

11 Use these verbs to rewrite four sentences from Exercise 9 so they mean the opposite. You may need to change more than just the verbs.

| damage | encourage | resolve | strengthen |

CONVERSATION PRACTICE

12 Work in pairs. Think of two proposals in areas such as those in the box below: one that you would both like to see happen, and one – either good or bad – that you have heard is happening. Discuss the possible consequences of each proposal.

| education | foreign policy | finance | health |
| housing | the economy | culture | transport |

13 Work with a new partner. Take turns to start conversations about the proposals. You can use the phrases below to start your conversations.

I don't know about you, but I'm personally in favour of …

Did you hear about this proposal to …?

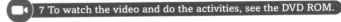 7 To watch the video and do the activities, see the DVD ROM.

NO LAUGHING MATTER

READING

1 **Work in groups. Discuss the questions.**

- Where do think the photo opposite was taken? What do you think is happening in the photo?
- Is film of politicians inside parliament shown on TV in your country? If yes, do you ever watch it?
- How do most politicians behave in parliament? What do you think of the way they behave?

2 **Read the article about Prime Minister's Questions in the UK Parliament. Then work in pairs and answer the questions.**

1 What happens in Prime Minister's Questions?
2 What does the author think of it?
3 What did you find most surprising / interesting in the article?
4 How far do you agree with the author's opinions?

3 **Based on what the author says, are the sentences true (T), false (F) or not mentioned (N)?**

1 The prime minister only attends parliament on a Wednesday.
2 MPs may exaggerate how funny they find the jokes during PMQs.
3 Satire was invented in the eighteenth century.
4 The main political parties share a similar approach to certain policies.
5 Satirical shows on TV encourage activism.
6 The author believes in the value of politics.
7 The Yes Men leak information that big companies would rather the media didn't see.
8 The author wants to abolish PMQs.

4 **Complete the sentences with the correct form of the words in bold in the article. The first one is done for you.**

1 There's still insufficient _representation_ of women in our parliament. Only 15% of MPs are women.
2 The Black Power movement that _____ in the 1960s grew out of the civil rights struggle in America.
3 A lot of young people are very _____ with politics but just not with the traditional parties.
4 They're not trying to undermine the whole system. They're _____ pointing out where there is corruption.
5 He has a very _____ following so he always attracts big crowds when he speaks.
6 They're very concerned with ensuring the security of _____ systems such as passports.
7 It's an old book but still funny and relevant today. It's a _____ of war and life in the army.
8 They _____ lowering the tax because they said it would only benefit the rich.

5 **Work in groups. Discuss the questions.**

- Is there anything similar to PMQs in your country?
- Do British politicians sound similar or different to politicians in your country? In what way?
- Are there any satirical programmes or satirists on TV in your country? If yes, do you watch them?
- What funny videos, images or short texts are doing the rounds on the Internet at the moment?
- Do you ever tell or make jokes? If yes, who with?

LISTENING

6 ▶ **12** **Listen to a joke about politicians. Decide:**

1 how funny you think it is on a scale of 1–5.
2 what aspect of politics it's joking about.
3 if you think there is an element of truth about it.

UNDERSTANDING VOCABULARY

'Ways of' verb groups

The person telling the joke used some descriptive verbs that show the way something was done.

He arrives at the gates of heaven **clutching** *his bags.* = hold (tightly)

He **strolls** *along the beach.* = go / move (on foot with leisure)

He **gazes** *at the beautiful sunset.* = look (with wonder)

He **gasps**, *'But what are you doing …'* = say (in shock)

His old friends are … **chattering** *to each other.* = talk (continuously)

The devil **chuckles** *…* = laugh (quietly)

These descriptive verbs are usually used with the same prepositions and with the same grammatical patterns as the more basic verbs such as *hold, move, look,* etc. Sometimes recognising these patterns can help you to guess unknown words.

7 **Work in pairs. Look at audio script 12 on page 105 and put the words in bold into groups according to their basic meaning.**

8 **Add these words to the groups you made.**

grab	glare	creep	race	mumble
giggle	mutter	stare	stagger	scream

9 **Work in pairs. You are going to tell each other a joke.**

Student A: read the joke in File 11 on page 97.

Student B: read the joke in File 12 on page 98.

Replace the words in italics with more descriptive words. Then tell the joke to your partner. Decide how you would rate each one on a scale of 1–5.

Symbol of democracy is a joke

There are some who say that Prime Minister's Questions (PMQs) is a great symbol of democracy. Every Wednesday the head of our government is forced to attend parliament and answer questions from MPs. As MPs are **representatives** of the people, PMQs offers a direct line of access to the top where we, the public, can hold the government to account for their actions. That's the theory. However, the reality is somewhat different and actually symbolises much that is wrong with politics here.

What usually happens is this: the leader of the main **opposition** party stands up and asks a question about a new policy or about some recently released figures that show the government is failing. I say asks a question, but half the time it's just a joke at the prime minister's expense. The prime minister then essentially ignores the question and pokes fun at the leader of the opposition, who then has to ask another question or say something funny. All of this is accompanied by MPs on both sides shouting or laughing like hyenas as they compete to demonstrate **loyalty** to their leader.

" What has this got to do with politics or democracy? "

Defenders of the ritual note that this type of humour has a long history in British politics. Records of politicians insulting each other in this manner date back to the eighteenth century. They also claim it engages voters in issues and represents the values of free speech. They even argue that such satirical humour prevents the **emergence** of dictators by using mockery and ridicule to reduce fear and build confidence.

While there may well be elements of truth in the historical claim, the bottom line is that what we are really seeing here is politics being turned into **mere** entertainment. The politicians actually *pay* professional comedy writers to write jokes for them, and the rest of the media love it because it fits neatly into

a five-minute slot on the TV news. This is not satire championing truth and exposing the corruption of power. It's more like kids in a playground throwing insults. The kids don't really mean it – it's just a game – and the same goes for the politicians. As 'opposing' parties have more or less adopted the same economic outlook, the only way to mark a difference is through this mock abuse.

And those comedy writers for PMQs are probably the same kind that write for the TV satirists, who the academic Russell Peterson says are undermining the value of politics. He argues that real satire adopts a moral stance – it has an agenda and seeks change – whereas most **satirical** TV programmes only seek balance. They aim to take the mickey equally out of *all* politicians based on character more than policy. As a result, *all* politicians are seen as bad and political **engagement** is discouraged.

But elsewhere it seems humour *can* engage voters. For example, a popular blog by the satirist Bepe Grillo in Italy led to the formation of a movement that gained 25% of the vote in the 2013 elections. And as can be seen from the exploits of the activist duo Jacques Servin and Igor Vamos – better known as the Yes Men – laughter can still pose a serious challenge to the rich and powerful. The pair have developed a technique they call '**identity** correction'. Posing as representatives of entities they dislike – the World Trade Organization, for instance, or the ExxonMobil oil and gas company – they issue shocking, ridiculous press releases that exaggerate official positions in order to force back into the news stories that corporations would rather bury. Whatever your politics, surely such tactics serve as a braver, better symbol of democracy than a couple of comfortable middle-aged white blokes exchanging empty insults once a week.

Comments 146　|　Add a comment　|　Share

CAST YOUR VOTE

READING

1 Work in groups. Discuss what you know about Switzerland. Think about the following:

- its geography
- its history
- famous Swiss people – living or dead
- its famous products, brands and services
- its political system

2 Read an article about the Swiss electoral system. Find:

1 three ways in which Swiss MPs are quite unusual.
2 three examples of how Swiss people participate in politics.
3 how members of the National Council and the Senate are selected.
4 one reason that may explain why not many Swiss people vote.

3 Read the article again. Tick (✓) what you think are positive aspects of the Swiss system. Cross (✗) what you think is negative.

4 Work in pairs. Compare and explain your ideas. Discuss what is similar to / different from the system in your country.

5 With your partner, discuss what you think the words and phrases in bold in the article mean.

VOCABULARY Elections and politics

6 Use these nouns to complete each group of phrases below. There are two nouns you do not need.

consensus	figure	party	scandal	victory
election	MP	poll	strike	vote

1 a prominent ~ in the anti-war movement / a hate ~ / be seen as a ~ of fun / a very influential ~
2 the ~ takes place in May / call an ~ / rig an ~ / in the run-up to the ~
3 carry out a ~ / conduct a ~ among students / in the latest ~ / go to the ~s
4 reach a ~ / establish a ~ / an emerging ~ / a broad ~
5 expose a bribery ~ / a sex ~ / be mixed up in a ~ / cover up a ~
6 stand as an ~ / lobby ~s / a right-wing ~ / an outspoken ~
7 a unanimous ~ / cast your ~ / a protest ~ / alleged ~-rigging
8 a narrow ~ / a landslide ~ / a hollow ~ / claim ~

7 Underline any phrases in Exercise 6 that are new for you. Write example sentences for each.

8 Work in pairs. Compare your sentences. Then think of one more verb or adjective that can be used with each of the ten nouns in the box in Exercise 6.

 ## THE ELECTORAL SYSTEM SWISS STYLE

Consisting of 26 cantons, or member states, the country of Switzerland has a long tradition of democracy – some claim it dates back to the 13th century. It is also perhaps unique in the amount of power it **allocates** to regional and local institutions. Parliament only sits 12 weeks a year and MPs are paid modest salaries compared to **counterparts** abroad. Most have second jobs in the community.

In fact, this devolution of power extends to individual citizens. Even when the national parliament decides to change **federal** law, individuals can challenge the decision by collecting 50,000 signatures on a **petition**. This triggers an automatic **referendum**. Furthermore, anyone can propose laws by getting 100,000 signatures. Similar processes exist at a local level. People may vote on these single issues 15 times a year or more. The vast majority of votes are cast by post.

The Swiss have a federal parliament with two bodies – the National Council and the Senate – which choose the government. The Senate is formed by the individual cantons electing two

representatives each, irrespective of population size. The 200 MPs in the National Council are elected via a complex form of **proportional representation**. Each canton is allocated a number of seats according to population, ranging from 34 (Zurich) to one (Uri). The political parties provide lists of candidates for each canton, which are sent to the electorate. Voters can vote not only for the party but also for specific candidates. They can even make their own list.

The number of seats each party gains in any canton is determined by the percentage of party **ballot papers** returned. The specific people who are then chosen for each party depends on the individual votes cast for each candidate. Because of this system, individual representatives maintain a direct relationship with their voters, often rejecting **the party line**. Special interest groups often **lobby** voters to support MPs favouring their cause.

Coalitions are the norm in Switzerland as parties don't gain an absolute majority, with the result that a tradition of **consensus** has become established. This may partly explain why voter turnout is often less than 50% of the electorate.

LISTENING

9 Work in groups. Answer the questions below about these events.

an election for a student council	a referendum
a general election	a strike ballot
a local election	a talent show vote
an opinion poll	a vote in parliament

1 In which of the above do you vote for a person or party? In which for a law or action?

2 Who votes in each case?

3 Which ones have you voted in and why? What was the outcome?

4 Which one of the above is the only event you don't directly vote in? How is it sometimes connected to voting?

5 Can you think of any other times you might vote?

6 Have you ever stood for election or campaigned in a vote? When? What happened?

10 ▶ **13** Listen to five people talking about events from Exercise 9. Match each speaker (1–5) to one of the events.

11 ▶ **13** Listen again. Match each speaker to one of the following. There is one that you do not need.

Which person:

a mentions a broken promise?

b talks about vote-rigging?

c talks about voter turnout?

d talks about standing for parliament?

e expresses surprise at something?

f is defending an unpopular decision?

People in Glarus, Switzerland continue their 700-year tradition of open-air voting

GRAMMAR

Conditionals 2

Conditionals can be used to talk about:

1 general past truths.

2 imagined events in the past.

3 imagined events in both the past and the present.

12 Match the sentences from the listening (a–e) to the functions (1–3) in the box. Then work in pairs and compare your ideas.

a It **helped** the programme's ratings if they **had** a kind of hate figure.

b I **might not have minded** so much if the calls **were** free, but they're making a fortune on them.

c If they **hadn't been** so reluctant to negotiate, we **would not be taking** this action now.

d If they**'d called** on another day, I **wouldn't have taken part**.

e It's unlikely we **would've abolished** uniforms if we **didn't have** a body like this.

G Check your ideas on page 90 and do Exercise 1.

13 With your partner, decide which option is *not* possible. Then discuss the difference in meaning between the two possible options.

1 If the parliamentary vote goes against the government next week, *it could trigger / it'll trigger / it triggered* an election.

2 The government should've done more for the middle classes if they *want / wanted / would've wanted* to win the election.

3 If they complain, *tell / I wouldn't tell / I told* the boss.

4 If I'd heard something, *I'd told / I would tell / I would've told* you.

5 If it hadn't been for him, I *wouldn't be working / wouldn't have been working / would never have got* a job here.

14 Think about the past and present results of the following things. Write two conditional sentences about each. Then work with your partner and compare your ideas.

• the result of the last election

• the impact a famous figure has had in your country

• an important moment in your life

G For further practice, see Exercise 2 on page 91.

SPEAKING

15 Work in groups. Discuss the questions.

• What's voter turnout like in your country? Why?

• How do you think democracy could be improved?

• Which elections were significant for you personally / your country / the world? Why?

• Have you heard of any scandals? What happened?

• What would be your proposals if you stood for a school body / a local election / parliament?

VIDEO 2

SONGLINES
OF THE ABORIGINES

1 **Work in groups. Discuss these questions.**
- What do you think of the painting in the photo?
- Do you think the painting represents anything – or is it just abstract?
- What do you know about the Aborigines in Australia?

2 ▶️ **8** **Watch the video. Are the sentences true (T), false (F) or not mentioned (N)?**
1 Aborigines were one of the first groups to move from Africa.
2 Traditional Aboriginal culture still exists today.
3 Aborigines used to have innovative farming techniques.
4 By the mid-20th century, the Aborigine population had halved in size.
5 The decision to settle in towns had a negative impact on Aboriginal culture.
6 Songlines serve both a practical and symbolic function.
7 You can purchase maps of the routes that the Songlines take across Australia.
8 The Dreaming allows Aborigines to maintain contact with their ancestors.

3 ▶️ **8** **Work in pairs. Try to complete the sentences about the video with a noun in each space, then watch again and check your answers.**
1 Aboriginal culture survives today in remote _____ of the outback.
2 In a sense, Arnhem Land is the _____ of Aboriginal culture.
3 European _____ to 'civilise' the Aborigines had tragic _____.

4 There have always been strong spiritual _____ to the landscape in Aboriginal culture.
5 Aboriginal beliefs are founded on a deep _____ for and _____ to the land.
6 Walking the Songlines is a way of tracing the _____ of their ancestors.
7 Songlines mark _____ between different _____.
8 They also represent a spiritual _____.

4 **Work in pairs. Discuss the questions.**
- Did the video give you any further thoughts about the painting above?
- What did you find surprising / unsurprising / interesting / depressing? Why?
- Do you know of any other indigenous groups? How strong is their culture today?
- How important do you think rituals are in everyday life? Give some examples.

UNDERSTANDING FAST SPEECH

5 ▶️ **9** **Listen to an extract from the video said at natural pace. Try to write down what you hear. Then compare your ideas with a partner.**

6 ▶️ **10** **Try again. This time you will hear a slower version of the extract.**

7 **Check your ideas in File 10 on page 98. Groups of words are marked with / and pauses are marked //. Stressed sounds are in CAPITALS. Practise saying the extract.**

REVIEW 2

GRAMMAR AND UNDERSTANDING
VOCABULARY

1 Complete the email with one word in each space. Contractions count as one word.

Dear Claude,
Thanks for the wedding invitation. I ¹_____ have replied ²_____ thing, but I wasn't sure I could get time off and what ³_____ one thing and another it's taken longer than I thought to sort out. Anyway, I'd love to come. The only thing ⁴_____ is still uncertain ⁵_____ whether Maddie can come too. I know you said the wedding was ⁶_____ big thing, but we would really like to buy you something special. The main ⁷_____ Maddie and I got together ⁸_____ that you introduced us. It wouldn't feel right if we ⁹_____ get you anything – and it's not as ¹⁰_____ we can't afford it.
James

2 Complete the second sentence so that it has a similar meaning to the first sentence using the word given. Do not change the word given. You must use between four and five words, including the word given.

1 There's not much to see there except maybe the ruined castle.
The only _____ the ruined castle. **WORTH**

2 If it wasn't seen as inappropriate here, I would've gone with you.
I would've gone with you, but it _____ here. **DONE**

3 It's just been a series of unfortunate events that's caused this mess.
I wouldn't be in this mess if one thing _____. **ANOTHER**

4 He just looks endlessly at the screen and pretends to work.
All _____ the screen and pretend to work. **STARE**

5 I'm glad it wasn't me because I always laugh uncontrollably in those situations.
I wouldn't have been able to _____ been me. **GIGGLING**

6 He always speaks very unclearly, which is very annoying.
What annoys me _____ all the time. **MUMBLES**

3 Choose the correct option.

1 Me? Have a holiday? Chance would be a *fine / good* thing.

2 I *staggered / glared* home at about six in the morning.

3 He *muttered / screamed* something under his breath.

4 I could've helped if you had ever *ask / asked*.

5 I saw something *scamper / grab* across the kitchen floor.

6 What concerns me is the *number / amount* of crime in the area.

VOCABULARY

4 Decide if these adjectives refer to society, politicians or both.

hypocritical	family-centred	outspoken
secular	conservative	male-dominated
right-wing	liberal	powerful
welcoming	diverse	ruthless

5 Match the verbs (1–10) with the collocates (a–j).

1	flush	a	a carpet / the foundations
2	load	b	my jeans / up the contract
3	lay	c	the table / your feet
4	rip	d	the toilet / the pipes out
5	wipe	e	my shirt / his reputation
6	sweep	f	the result / the election
7	stain	g	the floor / to power
8	unblock	h	the top shelf / a broad consensus
9	rig	i	the sink / the drain
10	reach	j	the dishwasher / the rifle

6 Complete the sentences. Use the word in brackets to form a word that fits in the space.

1 If you ask me, our society is far too _____. (bureaucracy)

2 I'm against laws to restrict the Internet. I think they are _____. (work)

3 There continues to be a lack of social _____ in our country. (mobile)

4 The _____ for the economy is not very bright. (look)

5 The _____ of Internet start-ups is threatening traditional businesses. (emerge)

6 I haven't read the book so I can't pass _____ on it. (judge)

7 She was a very _____ figure in the feminist movement. (influence)

8 We should _____ the power of the police. (strong)

7 Complete the text with one word in each space. The first letters are given.

We are going to have a general election here soon. The election was ¹tr_____ by a huge bribery scandal that was ²ex_____ in the press. Several ministers were ³m_____ u_____ in it, but the government had tried to ⁴c_____ it u_____. In the last election, the governing party won a ⁵la_____ victory, but all the latest ⁶p_____ suggest they've lost a lot of support. The main opposition party also has a new leader who has been a ⁷pr_____ figure in the fight against corruption and is seen as having a lot of ⁸ch_____, which is attracting many new voters. The only thing in the government's ⁹fa_____ is that they have succeeded in ¹⁰bo_____ the economy after it was devastated by a banking crisis. That's obviously ¹¹be_____ a lot of people so they could still win. I don't know where I ¹²st_____ yet. I might not vote at all!

5

GOING OUT, STAYING IN

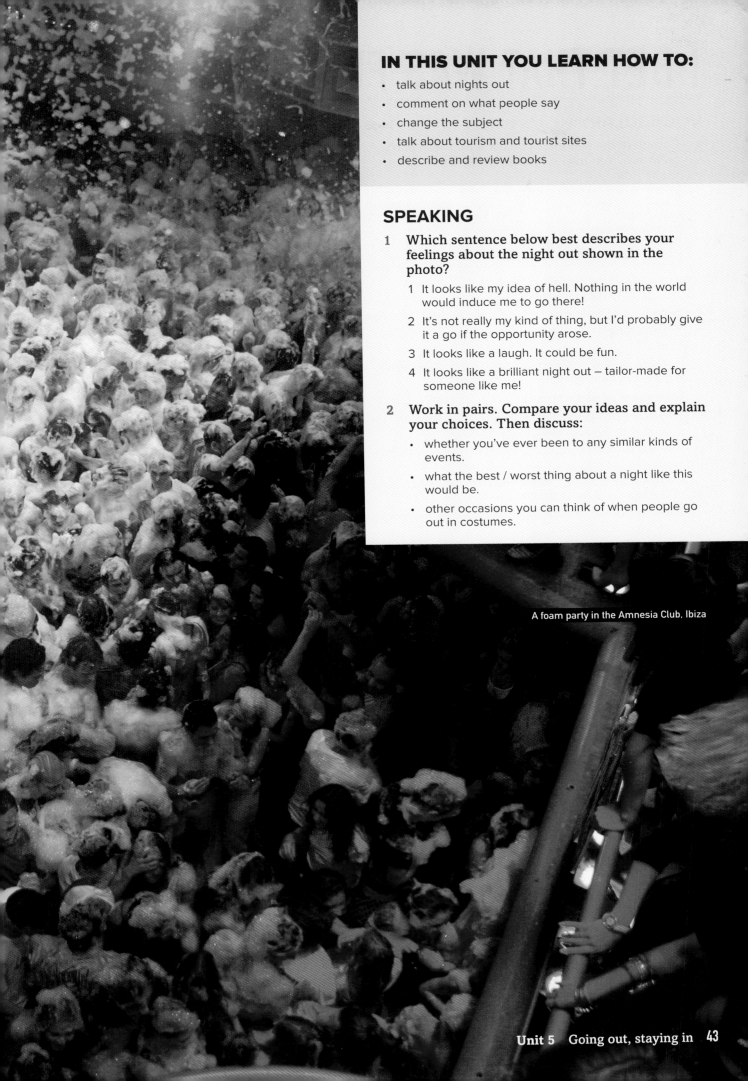

IN THIS UNIT YOU LEARN HOW TO:

- talk about nights out
- comment on what people say
- change the subject
- talk about tourism and tourist sites
- describe and review books

SPEAKING

1   Which sentence below best describes your feelings about the night out shown in the photo?

   1   It looks like my idea of hell. Nothing in the world would induce me to go there!

   2   It's not really my kind of thing, but I'd probably give it a go if the opportunity arose.

   3   It looks like a laugh. It could be fun.

   4   It looks like a brilliant night out – tailor-made for someone like me!

2   Work in pairs. Compare your ideas and explain your choices. Then discuss:

- whether you've ever been to any similar kinds of events.
- what the best / worst thing about a night like this would be.
- other occasions you can think of when people go out in costumes.

A foam party in the Amnesia Club. Ibiza

I BET THAT WAS FUN

VOCABULARY Nights out

1 Complete the sentences below with these pairs of words. You may need to change the order of the words.

awkward + scene	disappointment + hype
bits + floods	do + rough
bored + yawning	hilarious + stitches
burst + courses	mortified + swallow
crawl + exhausted	overwhelmed + tears

1 It was awful. I just couldn't stop _____. I was _____ out of my mind!

2 I'm _____! I didn't _____ into bed until after four.

3 She was so _____ by it all that she actually burst into _____.

4 There must've been at least ten _____. Honestly, I thought I was going to _____!

5 We were all on the floor in _____. It was _____!

6 Honestly! I was absolutely _____. I just wanted the ground to open up and _____ me!

7 It was such a _____. It really didn't live up to the _____.

8 I feel a bit _____ today. I had a big work _____ last night and didn't get home till two.

9 It was awful. He was in _____ when he heard – just in _____ of tears.

10 It caused a bit of a _____, actually. It was really quite _____, to be honest.

2 Choose the four words / phrases from Exercise 1 that you think you will use most often. Then decide if there are any words or phrases you don't think you will ever use. Think about why.

3 Work in pairs. Compare the words and phrases you chose for Exercise 2 and explain your ideas.

4 With your partner, think of a situation in which you might:

1 find yourself bored out of your mind.
2 be so overwhelmed that you burst into tears.
3 end up on the floor in stitches.
4 be absolutely mortified.
5 find that something doesn't live up to the hype.
6 go to a do.
7 end up in floods of tears.
8 witness a bit of a scene.

LISTENING

5 ▶ 14 Listen to two conversations. Answer the questions about each conversation.

1 What kind of night out do they talk about?
2 What other main topic do they discuss?

44

6 ▶ **14** Listen again. Which words and phrases from Exercise 1 are used in each conversation?

7 Complete the sentences from the conversations with the correct prepositions or adverbs. Then look at audio script 14 on page 105 and check your answers.

Conversation 1

1 She's been _____ a lot recently.

2 She soon got _____ it.

3 They went _____ really, really well.

4 He's so full _____ himself, that guy.

5 Hey, talking _____ dancing, are you still going to those tango classes?

6 I'm still a bit prone _____ treading on toes.

Conversation 2

7 It's all _____ hand.

8 It's just that I could do _____ it at the moment.

9 I've got far too much _____.

10 Thanks for being so _____ top of things.

11 Oh, _____ the way, how was your meal the other night?

12 This guy at a table in the corner just suddenly burst _____ screaming at one of the waiters.

8 Work in groups. Discuss the questions.

- Have you ever been to a surprise party? How was it?
- When was the last time you had a very late night? Why?
- How do you usually celebrate your birthday?
- Do you like dancing? What do you usually dance to?
- When was the last time you went out for a meal? Where did you go? What was it like?
- Have you ever complained in a restaurant? If so, why?

DEVELOPING CONVERSATIONS

Commenting on what is said

We use *I bet / imagine*, *must / must've* and *can't / can't have* to comment on what is said.

I bet she was pleased. (= I'm fairly sure she was.)

You must be getting quite good, then. (= I'm fairly sure you are getting good.)

That must've been quite filling!

That can't have been much fun.

We usually respond to comments like these by showing whether we think the comments are accurate or not and then adding follow-up comments of our own.

B: *You must be getting quite good, then.*

A: *I wouldn't go that far. I'm still a bit prone to treading on toes.*

C: *That must've been quite filling!*

D: *It was. I was ready to burst by the end of it all.*

9 Use *must / can't* to rewrite the comments below without changing the basic meaning.

1 I bet that was pretty dull, wasn't it?

2 I bet you're not feeling your best at the moment, are you?

3 I don't imagine he was very pleased when he found out.

4 I imagine you're glad you didn't go now.

5 That must've cost a fortune.

6 She can't have been feeling very well.

7 Judging from his accent, he must be foreign.

8 You can't be serious!

10 ▶ **15** Listen and check your ideas. Which comments in Exercise 9 were accurate, according to the way the other person responded?

11 Work in pairs. Choose four rewritten comments from Exercise 9. Decide what you think was said before each one and how the comments could be responded to if they are accurate – and if they're not.

A: *The guy sitting next to me spent the whole evening talking about golf.*

B: *Wow! That must've been pretty dull.*

A: *Yeah, it was. I had to stop myself from yawning. / You'd think so, wouldn't you, but he was actually pretty funny about it all.*

CONVERSATION PRACTICE

12 Choose one of these tasks.

a Think of a memorable night out you have had. Think about where you went, who with, what it was like, what happened, how you felt, what time you got home, etc.

b Invent a night out. You can imagine it was an amazing night or an awful one. Decide where you went, who with, what it was like, what happened, etc.

13 Now work in pairs. Tell each other about your nights out. Try to use as much language from this lesson as you can. Your partner should ask questions and add comments while listening.

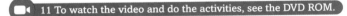
11 To watch the video and do the activities, see the DVD ROM.

OFF THE BEATEN TRACK

READING

1 Work in pairs. List as many famous sites and things to do in London as you can. Then share your ideas with the class. Which places / things to do sound best? Why?

2 Read the introduction to an article about visiting London and explain:

1 the title of the article.

2 what kind of impression of London the writer thinks tourists are getting.

3 Read the rest of the article. Match the headings (a–h) to the parts of the article (1–6). There are two headings you do not need.

a Festive food
b Free view
c Far out night out
d Leisurely stroll
e True insights
f East End playhouse
g Not just chippies
h Quiet night out

4 Work in pairs. Try to remember how the words and phrases in italics were expressed in the article. Then read the article again and check your answers.

1 had never *risked going outside of* Zone 1

2 *people go swimming throughout the year*

3 if you're *a bit hungry*

4 it also *keeps and displays* a collection of household objects

5 *Charlie Chaplin once performed at the theatre*

6 *a typical kind of show in Britain*

7 we've *happily accepted a large variety* of international food

8 it's *almost impossible to logically choose* where to go

9 was *known for being socially deprived*

10 after the usual family visitors *have gone to* bed

5 Work in pairs. Discuss the questions.

- Which two recommendations most appeal to you? Why?
- Which places don't interest you? Why?
- What's the best museum you've been to? What's the most unusual one?

UNDERSTANDING VOCABULARY

Noun + of

In the article, you saw several nouns with *of*. They may describe:

- a group (*herd of cows*).
- number / amount (*all manner of*).
- a part (*the rear of the building*).
- the content (*photographs of domestic life*).
- the thing that was done (*performances of everything from stand-up comedy to opera*).
- the feeling something gives (*the weirdness of a silent disco*).

6 Match the nouns + *of* (1–8) to their endings (a–h) to make noun phrases.

1 sign of   a goods / blood / labour
2 tip of   b reading / eating / their company
3 floods of   c mosquitoes / flies / wasps
4 bunch of   d the EU / jobs / a new art form
5 swarm of   e life / things to come / weakness
6 pleasure of   f my tongue / the iceberg / the pen
7 supply of   g flowers / mates / stuff to do
8 creation of   h complaints / tears / enquiries

7 Work in pairs. Choose a noun phrase from each of the groups in Exercise 6 and make sentences that are true.

GRAMMAR

Noun phrases

We can add a lot of information before and after a main noun in different ways.

A walk will lead to a panorama.

*A **ten-minute** walk **up a steep path** will lead to an **amazing** panorama **of London**.*

8 Work in pairs. Look at the underlined noun phrases in the article. Match each noun phrase (1–9) to one of the ways information is added (a–i).

a adding a name of something to the kind of thing it is

b adding a noun before the main noun to describe it

c adding several adjectives

d using a number + noun compound adjective

e adding a prepositional phrase to show a feature

f a relative clause

g a reduced relative clause using a present (*-ing*) participle

h a reduced relative clause using a past participle

i a reduced relative clause using an adjectival phrase

G Check your ideas on page 91 and do Exercises 1 and 2.

9 Work in pairs. Add information to the subjects and objects in these sentences. Which pair in the class can write the longest correct noun phrases in each case?

1 The museum houses a collection.

2 Man seeks woman.

3 A man has won a prize.

10 With your partner, decide two places to contribute to 'A hidden guide to …' about a city / town you both know. Write two short paragraphs in a similar style to the article. Use extended noun phrases.

G For further practice, see Exercises 3 and 4 on page 92.

A hidden guide to London

Hampstead Heath

DON'T BE A SHEEP! Seeing tourists being guided around London like herds of sheep, you do wonder what impression of London they're getting. They queue for hours outside Madame Tussauds to see a waxwork of Cristiano Ronaldo, eat in the Hard Rock Café, race round the British Museum looking at mummies from Egypt, then buy a postcard of the Queen and London is done. Paris, here we come! I met a foreign businessman recently who'd been coming to London every year for 20 years but had never ventured beyond Zone 1 on the underground or the classic sites. Come on, people! London has so much more to offer! So let's tempt you off the beaten track and leave the hordes of tourists behind.

1   Forget spending a small fortune climbing The Shard in central London – hop on a C2 bus and go to Parliament Hill. A ten-minute walk up a steep path will lead to an amazing panorama of London – on a clear day, anyway. And if it's not clear, you can still stroll round [1]Hampstead Heath with its natural ponds, where some go for a dip all year round. Alternatively, visit [2]the 18th-century stately home, Kenwood House, with its fine collection of art. And if you're feeling peckish, they serve classic English [3]cream teas.

2   Yeah, the British Museum is great, but as more than one person has pointed out, it's not very British. So if you really want to see how we've lived through the ages, you should check out the [4]Geffrye Museum, which contains eleven living rooms from different periods of history. It also houses a collection of household objects and photographs of English domestic life. At the rear of the building, there are four period [5]gardens showing changing trends in that most British of pastimes, gardening.

3   There are all manner of performance spaces outside the West End, but we've chosen The Hackney Empire, a theatre that once hosted Charlie Chaplin. Today, you can see performances of everything from stand-up comedy to opera, but it's perhaps best known for its award-winning Christmas pantomimes. The pantomime is a peculiarly British show loosely based around a fairy tale, with audience participation and satirical jokes, and where the leading man is a woman and the main comic woman character is a man!

4   They say British cuisine is dreadful, which is why we've embraced a huge array of international food. That said, even supposedly typical British dishes like fish and chips originally came from Europe, so perhaps things have always been this way. We'd say it's a toss-up where to go for [6]our best multicultural cheap eats. Go north to Harringay for the best Turkish kebabs. Another option would be to head west to Southall for top South Indian food. While you're there, you could even do [7]a six-hour course with Monisha, where you'll tour the local shops for produce and learn to cook the best curry. And if you really want fish and chips? Toffs of Muswell Hill is a classic [8]'chippie' run by second-generation Greek immigrants!

5   There was a time that Dalston was synonymous with social deprivation, drugs and crime. These days, it's known as one of the hippest [9]places in town, full of trendy bars and restaurants, underground clubs and cool young things hanging out. The only problem is, there's no tube station so it takes a while to get there.

6   So it's not exactly off the beaten track – it's London Zoo – but it sneaks into our list for its great Zoo Late evenings, held throughout the summer after the usual family visitors are tucked up in bed. As well as seeing the animals under the stars, you can enjoy live stand-up and the cool weirdness of a silent disco in which everyone wears headphones (silent apart from some tuneless singing along!).

The Hackney Empire

Cooking curries in London

Unit 5   Going out, staying in   **47**

IT CAME HIGHLY RECOMMENDED

SPEAKING

1 Work in groups. Discuss the questions.

- Look at the photo of a book club meeting. What do you think it involves?
- Do you know anyone who belongs to either a real-world book club or an online one?
- Can you think of three reasons why people might join book clubs?
- What was the last thing you read? Would you recommend it? Why? / Why not?
- How do you usually decide what to read next?

LISTENING

2 ▶ 16 Listen to a radio feature about the explosive growth of book clubs. Find what evidence is given of:

1 Mark Zuckerberg's eccentric resolutions.
2 the difference that the page *A Year of Books* makes to sales.
3 how *A Year of Books* is in keeping with cultural trends.
4 how face-to-face reading groups have thrived.
5 how book clubs can result in increased sales.
6 opposition to the boom in book club membership.
7 the seemingly universal appeal of book clubs.

3 ▶ 16 Match the verbs (1–8) to the words they were used with in the radio feature (a–h). Then listen again and check your answers.

1	vow	a	a marked influence on reading choices
2	get through	b	these trends in a positive light
3	make	c	the power of Facebook
4	have	d	a book every fortnight
5	pick	e	to learn Mandarin Chinese
6	factor in	f	the spread of communal reading
7	see	g	six books a year
8	halt	h	a huge difference to sales

4 Work in groups. Discuss the questions.

- What do you think about Mark Zuckerberg and his resolutions?
- Is reading a big thing in your country? How does it manifest itself?
- Who do you think has the most influence on popular taste in your country? Why?
- Is the influence they have more positive or negative? In what way?
- Have you ever bought anything because of an online recommendation? If so, what?

VOCABULARY Describing books

5 Choose the correct option to complete the book reviews below.

6 Underline any phrases in the book reviews that are new for you. Then compare what you chose with a partner and discuss what they mean.

7 With your partner, discuss the questions.
- Have you read any of the five books? If you have, do you agree with the review?
- If not, which of the books would you most / least like to read? Why?
- Have you ever read anything similar to any of the books described?

SPEAKING

8 Imagine your class has started a book club. Think of the book you would most like other students to read. Who is it by and what is it called? Decide how to describe it. Use some of the language from Exercise 5.

9 Work in groups. Take turns to explain why your book is so good and try to persuade your partners to read your choice first. Then vote to decide which book to read first.

 The Son *Jo Nesbo*

This crime thriller ¹*centres / revolves* on a young man in prison for confessing to crimes he didn't commit. The novel starts slowly, but the pace picks up as the ²*argument / plot* develops. With a ³*star / protagonist* who remains thoroughly likeable despite his flaws and its crisp, credible ⁴*dialogue / speech*, there's much to enjoy here.

2 Lies My Mother Never Told Me
Kaylie Jones

In this moving ¹*memoir / memory*, Jones confronts her childhood and her troubled relationship with her abusive mother, whose ²*conflict / struggle* to overcome her alcoholism is explored in heart-wrenching detail. The book ³*treats / deals* with the themes of acceptance and transcendence and is a real page-turner from start to finish. I can't ⁴*suggest / recommend* it highly enough.

3 The Hunger Games *Suzanne Collins*

¹*Sorting out / Tackling* such issues as poverty and oppression and ²*basing / revolving* around a televised survival game in which kids fight to the death, this may seem an unlikely best-seller. However, as it ³*traces / discovers* the influence that society has on the young, it manages to function as a gripping read while also ⁴*exploring / finding* teenage identity.

 Katherine *Anya Seaton*

This vivid portrayal of love and politics in medieval England is ¹*rooted / based* on a true story and manages to ²*bring / carry* its characters and era to life through its rich, vibrant language. If you believe that love conquers all and enjoy stories ³*held / set* in the past, then this uplifting ⁴*history / tale* may well be for you.

BOOK OF THE WEEK

"CONSTANT SUSPENSE . . . I COULDN'T STOP READING"
STEPHEN KING

THE HUNGER GAMES

SUZANNE COLLINS

5 Things My Girlfriend and I Have Argued About *Mil Millington*

This comic novel is so frequently laugh-out-loud funny that you might not want to read it in public! Told in the ¹*main / first* person, the book explores the many arguments between the ²*narrator / commentator* and his German girlfriend – to hysterical effect! By ³*turns / episodes* absurd, dark and full of ⁴*insight / judgment*, it's a must-read for anyone who's ever been in a relationship!

6

CONFLICT AND RESOLUTION

IN THIS UNIT YOU LEARN HOW TO:

- handle arguments in a constructive manner
- defend and excuse positions and behaviour
- talk about how you'd like things to be different
- discuss conflict and resolution
- understand and use extended metaphors

SPEAKING

1 **Work in pairs. Discuss the questions.**

- What do you think the relationship is between the people in the photo? Why?
- What do you think they might be arguing about? What might they be saying?
- Which sentences about arguing below do you agree with? Why?
  - It's healthy to let off steam every once in a while.
  - As soon as you lose your temper, you lose the argument.
  - Sometimes people need a good row to clear the air.
  - Arguing can become addictive and can have a terrible impact on relationships.
  - Raising your voice is a form of aggression.
  - An argument may be unpleasant, but it's often the first step towards a solution.

2 **Work with a new partner. Look at the things people often argue about below. Discuss how each might lead to an argument and the kinds of things that might be said during each argument.**

careers	politics	silly annoyances
exes	religion	household chores
homework	sport	stress and tiredness
in-laws	kids	time spent together
money	work	

3 **Which three things above do you think generally cause the worst arguments? Why?**

Accusations and recriminations

CLEAR THE AIR

VOCABULARY
Arguments and discussions

1 Make phrases people may use in arguments by putting the words in brackets in the correct order.

1 I hear what you're saying, but _____ (my / point / view / see / it / try / from / to / of).

2 That's not what I meant at all. _____. (words / my / you're / twisting)

3 _____. (our / crossed / I / we've / got / think / wires) That wasn't my intention at all.

4 Hey, chill! _____. (there's / voice / no / to / raise / need / your) I can hear you perfectly well.

5 I've obviously done something to upset you, so _____ (I / clear / we / think / air / should / the).

6 OK. You've made your point and I heard you. _____? (just / now / on / can / we / move)

7 _____. (wrong / sorry / out / came / all / that) Just pretend I didn't say that.

8 Alright! Calm down! _____! (world / it's / not / end / of / the / the)

9 It's done. Just forget about it. _____. (milk / no / there's / crying / spilt / over / point)

10 We're getting nowhere here. _____. (circles / going / just / round / we're / in) Can we just agree to disagree?

2 Work in pairs. For each phrase, decide:

1 whether it could be translated directly into your language.

2 whether you think saying this would calm an argument or make things worse – and why.

3 Look at these other phrases used in discussions. What word can complete all of them?

1 What's the _____ you're trying to make?

2 Doesn't that prove my _____?

3 I think you're missing the _____.

4 OK. Fair enough. I take your _____.

5 I wish you'd just get to the _____.

4 Work in pairs. Close your books. How many of the fifteen phrases from Exercises 1 and 3 can you remember?

5 Work in groups. Think of a time you might have said one of the following. Then tell each other what happened.

1 There's no point crying over spilt milk.

2 I think we've got our wires crossed.

3 Just pretend I didn't say that.

4 We're going round in circles.

5 I take your point.

LISTENING

6 ▶ **17** Listen to two conversations in which arguments occur. What is the main problem between the two people in each conversation?

7 ▶ **17** Decide if the following refer to Conversation 1, Conversation 2 or neither. Then listen again and check your answers.

Someone:

a has tripped over.

b has lost business.

c says they're very busy.

d says something sarcastic.

e has failed to pass on a message.

f takes offence.

g has spent money they didn't have.

h deliberately broke something.

i has had a series of difficulties over the day.

j was annoyed about a previous conversation.

8 Work in pairs. Discuss the questions.

- How are the two arguments resolved?

- Do you think the underlying problems have actually been resolved? Why? / Why not?

- Do you know anyone who is untidy, sarcastic, a control freak or easily offended? Does it bother you? Why? / Why not?

- Have you ever had any recurrent arguments with anyone? What about? Did you resolve them eventually?

DEVELOPING CONVERSATIONS

Defending and excusing

We often use the patterns *It's not as though / if …* and *It's just that …* to defend and excuse our position and / or behaviour.

A: *I almost broke my neck!*

B: *OK. Sorry. **It's not as though** I did it deliberately. (= I didn't do it deliberately.)*

*It came out wrong. I'm sorry. **It's just that** it's been a long day and this was the last straw.*

9 Work in pairs. Complete these exchanges with your own ideas.

1 A: There's no need to shout!
  B: I know. I'm sorry. It's just that …

2 A: Why did you buy that?
  B: What's the problem? It's not as if …
  A: I know. It's just that …

3 A: Why can't someone else do it? It's not as though …
  B: I know. It's just that …

4 A: I didn't want to ask you.
  B: Why not? It's not as though …
  A: I guess. It's just that …

5 A: I can't believe you did that.
  B: It's not as though …

10 Work with a new partner. Practise reading out the exchanges in Exercise 9. You may need to give different responses depending on what your partner says.

GRAMMAR

Wish and *if only*

We often use *wish* or *if only* to talk about things we want to be different. As these are hypothetical ideas, we use past forms (as we do in some conditional sentences). In conversation, *wish* may be followed by only a modal / auxiliary verb.

11 Work in pairs. Complete the sentences from the conversations with one word in each space. Then explain the function of each of the gapped sentences.

1 A: If only you ¹_____ put things away properly! …
  B: I was going to take it to my room …
  A: Well, I wish you ²_____.

2 D: What? You're joking?
  C: I wish I ³_____.

3 C: I wish you ⁴_____ said something sooner.
  D: I ⁵_____ have, but you hardly come out of that office.

 Check your ideas on page 92 and do Exercise 1.

12 Choose three of the comments below. Write three-line dialogues based around them.

A: *I can't believe you left the keys at home!*
B: *I know, but I wish you would drop it!*
A: *I would if I hadn't reminded you three times to get them!*

1 I wish you would drop it!
2 I wish I had. The whole thing's a nightmare!
3 To be perfectly honest, I wish I didn't have to.
4 If only you'd mentioned that an hour ago!
5 I wish I could!
6 We wouldn't have if you hadn't been so keen!

13 Work in groups. Use different patterns with *wish* to tell your partners something:

1 you regret (not) doing.
2 you regret not being able to do.
3 you'd like to be different about your life.
4 you'd like to be able to do.
5 you'd like to be different in the world.
6 you'd like to be different about someone you know.

 For further practice, see Exercise 2 on page 92.

CONVERSATION PRACTICE

14 Work in pairs. You are going to roleplay two conversations.

Student A: read File 13 on page 97.

Student B: read File 14 on page 98.

Spend a few minutes planning what you are going to say and what language from this lesson you will use.

15 Now roleplay the conversations.

12 To watch the video and do the activities, see the DVD ROM.

WAR AND PEACE

READING

1 You are going to read an article about the growth of the academic subject Peace Studies. Look at the photo opposite and discuss the questions.

- What do you think these Peace Studies students are doing – and why?
- Have you ever heard of this subject before? What do you think it involves?
- What kind of work do you imagine it would help graduates get?
- Do you think it would be a good degree to do? Why? / Why not?

2 Read the article and answer the questions in your own words.

1 What is the Tolstoy Cup and how did it get its name?
2 What does Stephen Pinker claim has led to a reduction in the levels of violence?
3 How and why has the image of Peace Studies changed?
4 What kinds of topics does the subject cover?
5 What are the main goals of peacebuilding?

3 Work in pairs. Discuss why the writer:

1 begins by talking about the Tolstoy Cup.
2 mentions the results of previous matches.
3 tells us about Stephen Pinker's book.
4 quotes George Orwell.
5 mentions hippies, John Lennon and nuclear weapons.
6 talks about the content of Peace Studies courses and peacebuilding.
7 finishes by talking about the Peace Studies footballers.

4 Find the nouns or noun phrases that go with these adjectives in the article. Then work with your partner and think of true examples for five of these collocations.

annual	dramatic	aggressive	legitimate
notable	associated	former	lasting
historical	diverse		

5 Work in pairs. Discuss the questions.

- Can you think of any other notable peace campaigners? What were their main achievements?
- Do you believe Stephen Pinker's claim that we are less violent? Why? / Why not?
- How do you think the five factors he mentioned may have helped to reduce violence?
- Which factor do you think has had the biggest effect? Why?
- Which of the peacebuilding goals do you think is hardest to implement? Why?

VOCABULARY Conflict and resolution

6 Put each group of words into the most likely order they happen, starting with the words in bold.

1 **be invaded** / defend yourself / join forces / defeat the enemy / gain ground / lose ground
2 **tension rises** / negotiate a ceasefire / the conflict escalates / fighting breaks out / war rages
3 **be surrounded** / be under siege for weeks / run out of food / become a prisoner of war / surrender
4 **plant a bomb** / put on trial / arrest / cause casualties and fatalities / track down / claim responsibility
5 **plot to overthrow the president** / return to democracy / seize control of the country / suffer sanctions / stage a coup / undermine economic stability
6 **receive reports of human rights violations** / seek a UN resolution / withdraw troops / send in international troops / re-establish security
7 **declare a ceasefire** / restart negotiations / sign a peace agreement / begin negotiations / talks break down / achieve a resolution

7 Work in groups. Think of examples of the following and talk about them in as much detail as you can using some of the new vocabulary from Exercise 6.

- an invasion
- a civil war
- a terrorist attack
- a coup
- an international intervention
- a peace process

PEACE TO DEFEAT WAR YET AGAIN?

This weekend sees the renewal of one of the great college sports rivalries. No, not the Oxford-Cambridge boat race down the River Thames but rather the return of the Tolstoy Cup. Established as an annual event back in 2007, the Cup is a football match between students from the Department of Peace Studies at the University of Bradford and the Department of War Studies at King's College, London, and takes its name from the Russian author of the 1869 novel *War and Peace*.

Over the years, the Peace Studies teams have featured a suitably international range of players, including several women, and wear the names of notable peace campaigners such as M. L. King and Gandhi on the backs of their light blue shirts. In what could be seen as an ironic inversion of the world off the pitch, Peace has defeated War every single year except one.

In fact, though, as Stephen Pinker observed in his book *The Better Angels of Our Nature*, despite appearances to the contrary, violence is actually in decline in many domains, including military conflict, murder, torture, and the treatment of children, animals and minority groups. Pinker credits five main historical forces with having brought about this dramatic reduction: the growth of nation states and legal systems; the increasingly global nature of commercial transactions; an increased respect for the interests and values of women; the spread of mass media and greater human mobility; and the increased importance of reason, which he claims helps us to see violence as a problem that can be solved rather than as a battle that has to have a winner.

While football remains, as George Orwell once noted, 'the continuation of war by other means', the increasing desire to solve conflict by means other than war can be seen in the huge growth of Peace Studies and the changing attitudes towards it as an academic subject. When Bradford University opened the UK's first school of Peace Studies in 1973, the subject was seen as a fringe area of study and Peace Studies students were stereotyped as hippies prone to lazing around, hugging one another and listening to John Lennon while dreaming of how nice the world would be if only everyone could just get on. However, the 1970s and 1980s saw a huge increase in the number of nuclear weapons – brought about by the ongoing Cold War freeze in US-Soviet relations – and the associated threat of mass destruction served to accelerate the expansion of the subject. Now in the 21st century, there are study institutes all over the world and courses exploring an incredibly diverse range of topics.

So what do Peace Studies programmes cover? Well, everything from terrorism, poverty and social inequality to group dynamics and aggressive tendencies in human nature. Courses today stress the complexity of conflict and the way such global crises as hunger, climate change, resource shortages and so on all feed in. At the very heart of the subject lies peacebuilding, a notion which contains lessons for all of us as we seek to ensure the world our children inherit continues to be less violent than the one we were born into. Peacebuilding works to ensure the surrender of weapons and reintegration of former soldiers into society. At the same time, it encourages the creation of better infrastructure and of legitimate state institutions. Finally, it attempts to stimulate community dialogue, bridge building, broader economic development, and so on.

Having seen previous Peace Studies players striving to win the battle on the football field, I can only hope they bring the same desire to the fight for long-term, lasting peace once they graduate.

A WAR OF WORDS

UNDERSTANDING VOCABULARY

Extended metaphors

We create metaphors by exploiting basic word meanings in order to refer to something else – because we think these things share qualities. So we *spend money*, but then we also *spend time*. The idea that time is equivalent to money is extended to many other verbs (*waste, use, lose,* etc.).

1 **Work in pairs. Read the short article about another extended metaphor. Answer the questions.**

  1 In what areas of life do we use words connected with war?

  2 Do these metaphors exist in your language?

  3 Do you agree they could impact on attitudes and behaviour? If yes, how? If not, why not?

For most of us, war and conflict is not something we have experienced directly, yet they have become a major part of how we describe many aspects of our world.

Perhaps unsurprisingly, in sport we talk about *attacking* and *defending*. A team may even *lay siege to* the goal, while their opponents refuse to *surrender* their lead. However, similar language is also found in health and medicine, where people talk about *battling* cancer, and business, where a firm might *launch* an *aggressive* marketing *campaign*. It's used in court, where *hostile witnesses* and lawyers try to *destroy* each other's arguments, and in politics, where governments may try to *combat* poverty by *targeting* their efforts on certain groups, and protesters (like soldiers) may *march* to defend rights that are *under attack*.

Most of the time, we are probably unaware of these metaphors, but some argue they have an impact on attitudes and the way we behave in areas such as relationships, medicine and politics – and that we should seek to express our ideas in more constructive ways.

2 **Put these words into the correct place in the sentences below. The first one is done for you.**

army	challenging	defences	target
guns	~~war~~	bombarding	invasion
capture	battle		

1 They've been underlined engaged in a fierce price *war* ⟨ which has hit profits.

2 The party has recruited a huge of volunteers for the campaign.

3 They are desperately trying to attract female voters and have been them with messages seeking support.

4 They're gaining ground in the polls and hope to 20 new seats.

5 They have a huge sales force compared to ours so we have to really our efforts.

6 She has won her fight to stop the photos being published, which she said was an of privacy.

7 All the big are through to the semi-finals of the competition so it's going to be a tight battle to get through.

8 The fifth set became a of wills as both players tired and it was Murray who finally surrendered.

9 They've had to join forces to fight off new businesses that are their position in the market.

10 Tiredness can often reduce our against viruses that attack our bodies.

The New Zealand national men's rugby union team, known as the All Blacks, perform a *haka* (a Māori challenge) before each international match.

3 Work in pairs. Compare your answers. Decide which area of life is being discussed in each sentence.

4 Underline the words in each sentence that are part of the same metaphor. The first one is done for you.

5 With your partner, answer the questions.

1 What else can reduce your defences against a virus?

2 How can we combat poverty / disease / addiction?

3 Who are the big guns in sport in your country?

4 Have you ever had to battle for something? What? Did you win or give in?

5 What companies, political parties or ideas are gaining ground at the moment? Why?

LISTENING

6 Work in groups. You are going to hear four news stories based on the headlines below. Discuss what you think has happened. Try to use vocabulary from Exercises 1 and 2.

SOFT DRINK SPY TRIAL STARTS

TV presenter defends himself against harassment allegations

Government policy hit by victory for liberty groups

PEACE BREAKS OUT OVER PIG STATUE

7 ▶ **18** Listen to the four news stories and find out what actually happened. Then work in pairs and rank the stories from 1 (= least serious) to 4 (= most serious).

8 ▶ **18** Listen again. Which sentences are true?

1 a Dan Craddock has been found guilty of spying.

   b Mr Craddock was a manager for Pit-Pots.

   c Jazz Drinks has a bigger market share now.

2 a Jonas Bakeman is in danger of losing his job.

   b Bakeman spoke to the press and fully apologised.

   c Ms Campbell claims she didn't initiate the affair.

3 a A court decided people didn't have to submit to body scans at airports.

   b One lobby group funded the woman's defence.

   c The government has accepted the ruling.

4 a Pig farming is an important industry in Paulston.

   b Both sides in the dispute inflicted some kind of damage.

   c The sides agreed a settlement between themselves.

9 ▶ **19** Work in pairs. Try to complete the full noun phrases from the news stories. Then listen and check your answers.

1 The two companies have been engaged in a _____ battle _____.

2 ... to pass on information _____ and _____ for _____ year.

3 He released a statement _____.

4 She had been bombarded with emails and _____ messages _____.

5 Campaigners have claimed victory in their battle _____ in _____.

6 The scanners play a _____ role _____ the _____ terrorism.

7 ... a statue of St John of Bidshire, the _____ local farmer Tim Langford.

8 It stood as a _____ symbol of the _____ Paulston is famous.

10 Work in groups. Discuss in as much detail as you can any stories you've heard about the following:

- spying
- celebrity affairs
- court cases and appeals
- community disputes

SPEAKING

11 As a class, choose two of the following statements to debate. Then divide into groups – half the class will agree with the two statements and the other half will disagree.

- You should never negotiate with terrorists.
- There should never be international intervention in a country's internal affairs.
- Wars are a necessary evil.
- You can't win the war on drugs.
- Peaceful protests are the only ones that work.
- Companies are too concerned with market share and growth.
- There should be more restrictions on advertising.

12 In your group, prepare your ideas and think how you might knock down your opponent's arguments. Choose a spokesperson for your group.

13 Now have the debate about the first statement. The spokesperson for the 'for' group should speak for two minutes. Then the 'against' spokesperson should speak. When they have finished, anyone can comment or ask questions.

14 Repeat Exercise 13 with the other statement.

VIDEO 3

THE BRAILLE HUBBLE

1 **Work in pairs. Discuss the questions.**

- How do you feel when you look at photos like the one above? Why?
- Have you ever used a telescope? What did you look at?
- How much do you know about space?
- Do you ever watch TV programmes / films or read books about space?
- What do you think we can learn from the exploration of space?

2 **▢ 13 Watch the video about a book of photographs of space. Find out:**

1 who the book is aimed at.

2 how it works.

3 how the students have influenced the creation of the book.

3 **▢ 13 Work in pairs. Discuss your answers to the questions, then watch again and check your answers.**

1 Are all the students completely blind?

2 Why did the photo showing different gases cause problems?

3 What does author Noreen Grice believe the book can achieve?

4 How did the students' attitude to the images change? Why?

5 What was the biggest problem with the early images?

4 **Complete the sentences about the video with these nouns.**

| feel | prototype | room | way |
| place | ridges | sheet | window |

1 The photos have found their _____ into a classroom for visually impaired students.

2 Each photo is overlaid with a transparent plastic _____.

3 The plastic overlay is covered with raised dots and _____.

4 The images help people with vision loss get a _____ for the far reaches of space.

5 The images may help people to better grasp their _____ in the universe.

6 Feedback from the students helped to shape the _____ of the book.

7 Later versions of the images left more _____ to manoeuvre.

8 The Hubble Telescope images provide a _____ on the wonders of space.

5 **Work in groups. Discuss the questions.**

- Do you know of any special schools for people with disabilities?
- What are the pros and cons of educating people with disabilities in special schools?
- How easy do you think it is for people with disabilities to get work in your country?
- What facilities are there for people with disabilities in your town / city? How could they be improved?
- Can you think of any well-known deaf or blind people? How did they become famous?

UNDERSTANDING FAST SPEECH

6 **▢ 14 Listen to an extract from the video said at natural pace. Try to write down what you hear. Then compare your ideas with a partner.**

7 **▢ 15 Try again. This time you will hear a slower version of the extract.**

8 **Check your ideas in File 10 on page 98. Groups of words are marked with / and pauses are marked //. Stressed sounds are in CAPITALS. Practise saying the extract.**

REVIEW 3

GRAMMAR AND UNDERSTANDING
VOCABULARY

1 Complete the text with one word in each space.

I've always wished I ¹_____ get a book published and last month I finally ²_____. The book is a novel ³_____ an old woman ⁴_____ fights a six-year ⁵_____ to stop her home being destroyed by developers. The sales have been good, so let's hope that's a sign of things to ⁶_____ as I'd love to write full time. Unfortunately, ⁷_____ is fierce among authors and the publishers are also engaged in a price ⁸_____, so it's only really the ⁹_____ guns of fiction who make any money. If ¹⁰_____ I was one of them!

2 Complete the second sentence so that it has a similar meaning to the first sentence using the word given. Do not change the word given. You must use between three and five words, including the word given.

1 Many people emailed us complaining about the service.
We _____ about the service. **FLOODS**

2 When the Euro was created, prices rose in some countries.
Prices rose in some countries _____ Euro. **OF**

3 I don't think we have seen anything like the whole story.
Sadly, I think this is only _____. **TIP**

4 I hate how they're constantly sending me all these emails.
I wish they _____ all these emails. **BOMBARD**

5 It was a mistake not to work together earlier.
I wish we _____ earlier. **FORCES**

6 The course lasts two weeks and all the tutors are experts.
It's a _____ experts. **BY**

3 Choose the correct option.

1 I agreed to do it, but now I wish I *haven't / didn't / hadn't*.

2 The opposition are gaining *territory / ground / share* in the polls.

3 A huge *army / herd / swarm* of volunteers helped out during the Olympics.

4 The exhibition contains Chinese artifacts *date / dated / dating* back 3,000 years.

5 We took a guided tour *Jones Travel / from the hotel / featured actors*.

4 Change the information around the nouns in bold to create a new sentence.

The Oscar-winning director **Joel Riley**, whose latest documentary *Sick Life* is currently on release, **gives a talk** at the Barbican tonight, explaining his take on the current state of the film industry in the UK.

VOCABULARY

5 What is the connection between each set of words? Think of a verb or adjective collocation for each noun.

1 flaw / plot / protagonist / insight / memoir

2 siege / talks / sanction / casualties / ceasefire

6 Match the verbs (1–10) with the collocates (a–j).

1	explore	a	a bomb / the idea
2	plant	b	troops / the accusation
3	seek	c	the hype / my expectations
4	withdraw	d	the theme / English identity
5	raise	e	into bed / along the floor
6	clear	f	a scene / fatalities
7	twist	g	the air / the stage
8	crawl	h	my words / the top off
9	live up to	i	support / to solve the conflict
10	cause	j	your voice / your hand

7 Complete the sentences with a preposition in each space.

1 I was bored _____ _____ my mind.

2 Try and see it _____ my point of view.

3 Listen, there's no point crying _____ spilt milk.

4 I think we're just going round _____ circles here.

5 The story revolves _____ life in one London street.

6 He just burst _____ tears when I told him.

8 Complete the sentences. Use the word in brackets to form a word that fits in the space.

1 It's just silly _____ which set off most arguments. (annoy)

2 The whole region wants to seek a _____ to the conflict. (resolve)

3 No-one has claimed _____ for the bombing. (responsible)

4 Hopefully, the agreement will bring _____ peace. (last)

5 The experience was quite _____ – I couldn't speak. (overwhelm)

6 The president scored a _____ success in the negotiations. (note)

9 Complete the text with one word in each space. The first letters are given.

The other day I watched the 1964 film *Seven Days in May*. It ¹tr_____ the plot by some US generals to ²ov_____ the President after he ³s_____ an agreement with the Soviet Union to disarm. As debate ⁴ra_____ over the treaty, some generals see it as ⁵su_____ to the communists and un⁶_____ the security of the country, so they plan to ⁷st_____ a coup and ⁸se_____ control of the communication systems in order to stop the treaty's implementation. The film follows the race to ⁹t_____ d_____ all the plotters and ¹⁰de_____ them. I thought it was quite ¹¹gr_____ but my son was ¹²ya_____ most of the way through it!

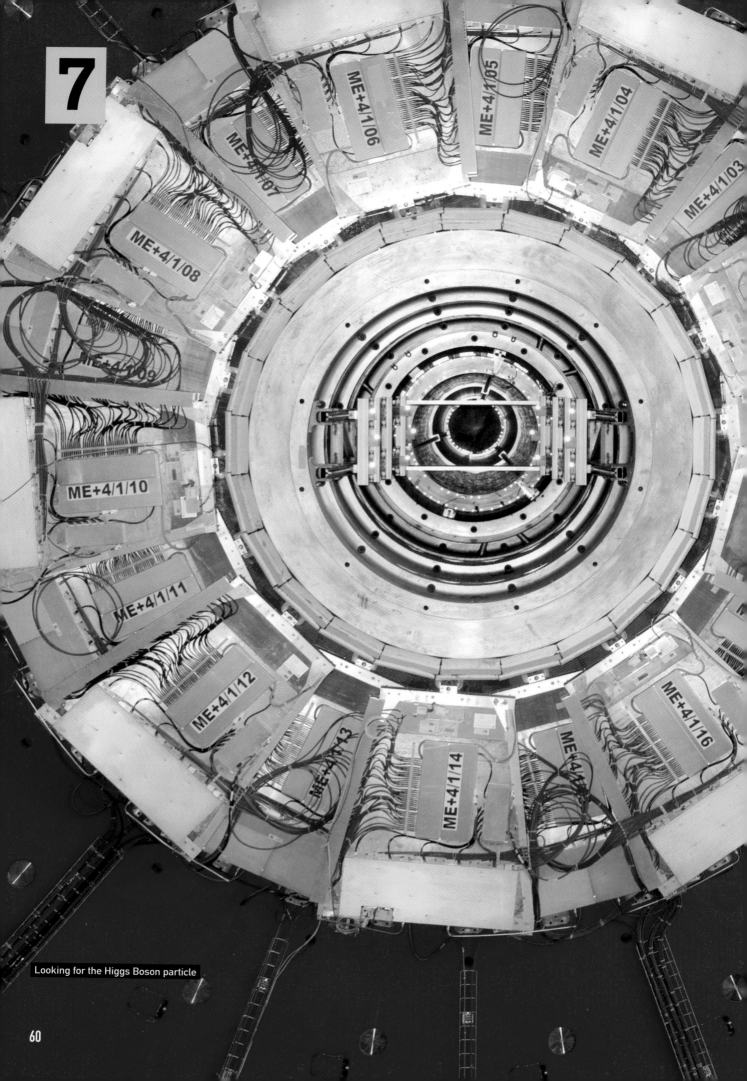

7

Looking for the Higgs Boson particle

IN THIS UNIT YOU LEARN HOW TO:

- discuss different areas of work in the field of science
- explain and discuss news stories about science
- express surprise and disbelief
- talk about science-fiction films
- form nouns and adjectives
- discuss the uses and abuses of statistics

SPEAKING

1 **Work in pairs. Discuss the questions.**

- The photo shows the Hadron Collider in Geneva. What do you know about its history, its size, what it is, how it works and what it's being used to research?

- Would you like to work in an environment like this? Why? / Why not?

- Do you know of any other major research projects going on anywhere in the world?

- To what degree do you see science as a force for good?

- What do you think are the most important scientific discoveries of recent times? Why?

2 **Work with a new partner. Discuss the questions.**

- Who are the most famous scientists you can think of? What are they famous for?

- What do you know about each of the different kinds of scientist below?

agricultural scientist	hydrologist
anthropologist	immunologist
astronomer	marine biologist
neurologist	military scientist
geologist	educational psychologist

- What's the main point of each job?

- Do you know anyone who works in the field of science? What do they do?

SCIENCE AND RESEARCH

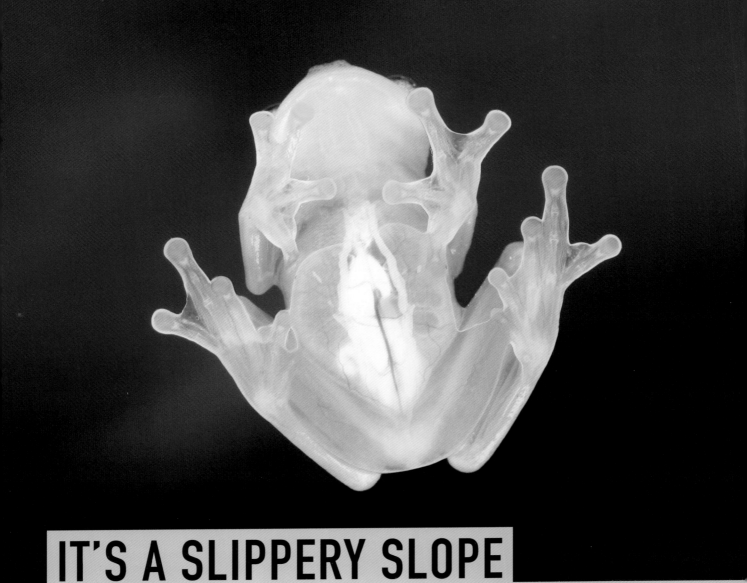

IT'S A SLIPPERY SLOPE

VOCABULARY Talking about science

1 **Replace the words and phrases in italics with the correct form of these synonyms.**

adverse	insert	carry out	remove
devise	reproduce	disorder	root
due	a slippery slope	lead to	step forward

1 It's a major *breakthrough* in the fight against AIDS.

2 They basically need to address the *underlying* cause of the phenomenon.

3 For his homework the other day, my son had to *extract* DNA from a banana.

4 They *stuck* probes into the brains of rats.

5 To me, this experiment represents *the thin end of the wedge*.

6 Researchers *undertook* the survey to establish a link between attitudes and health.

7 The findings could *pave the way for* new techniques.

8 Other scientists are yet to successfully *duplicate* the results under laboratory conditions.

9 The lack of funding was *down* to the radical nature of the theory.

10 There are concerns about *negative* side effects of the procedure.

11 The study found that the genetic *condition* was more prevalent than first thought.

12 Scientists have *created* a way to detect seismic waves before earthquakes hit.

2 **Work in pairs. Test each other.**

Student A: say the words and phrases in italics in Exercise 1.

Student B: close your books. Say the synonyms.

LISTENING

3 Work in pairs. Look at the newspaper headlines below. Discuss what you think each of these true stories is about. What research / experiments do you think may have been carried out in each case? What purposes might the results serve?

1 Hormone inhaler may help autism
2 Cat owners are more intelligent
3 Backing for space sun shield
4 Gay penguins adopt chick
5 DNA fragrance with the smell of Elvis Presley
6 Scientists breed see-through frogs and fish
7 Scientist gets funding for time-reversal experiment
8 Scientists successfully transplant mosquito nose

4 ▶ 20 Listen to two conversations about news stories related to the headlines in Exercise 3. Take notes on the stories.

5 Work in pairs. Compare your notes and check what you understood about each news story.

6 ▶ 20 Try to complete the sentences from the conversations with phrases. Then listen and check your answers.

Conversation 1

1 _____ do they do that?

2 They extract the DNA from the receptors, or something, and then insert it into the eggs. It's _____, really.

3 It sounds a bit peculiar, _____. I mean, what's the point?

4 A: They could use those smells to manufacture traps …
   B: OK. I suppose _____. I have to say, though, I still find all that gene manipulation a bit worrying.

5 B: One moment it's mosquito noses, the next they'll be engineering babies.
   A: _____! It's hardly the same thing!

Conversation 2

6 How on earth are they going to build something that big, _____ get it up there?

7 C: It'd take ten years to make.
   D: _____, then!

8 _____! What a waste of money!

9 C: They wouldn't have just made it up.
   D: Pah! _____ whether the whole climate change thing isn't all just a scam.

10 C: The evidence is pretty conclusive.
   D: _____?

7 Work in pairs. Discuss the questions.

- Which of the two stories you heard about is more important? Why?
- Do you have any concerns about genetic research?
- Is there any other kind of scientific research that you think is unethical?
- How far do you believe in climate change?
- Why do you think some people refuse to believe in things like climate change, despite fairly conclusive evidence?
- Are there any scientific theories that you – or people you know – are sceptical about? If so, why?

DEVELOPING CONVERSATIONS

Expressing surprise and disbelief

When we talk to people we know well, we can show surprise or disbelief by adding *on earth* to questions.

*How **on earth** do they do that?*

*How **on earth** are they going to build something that big?*

8 ▶ 21 Listen and repeat the questions. Pay attention to the stress and intonation.

9 Write questions using *on earth* in response to these comments.

1 We're developing a Nanobridge.
2 They've managed to grow a human ear on a rat's back.
3 Their head office is in Flitwick.
4 They're planning to send farm animals into space.
5 I've decided to take part in a drugs trial.
6 Apparently, they've bred see-through frogs to sell.

10 Work in pairs. Take turns to say the comments in Exercise 9. Your partner should respond with their question. Continue each conversation for as long as you can.

CONVERSATION PRACTICE

11 Work in groups of three. You are each going to read two true science news stories related to the headlines in Exercise 3.

Student A: look at File 15 on page 97.

Student B: look at File 16 on page 99.

Student C: look at File 17 on page 100.

Read your stories and make sure you understand them.

12 Now close your books. Take turns to start conversations by saying *Did you read that thing about …?* Your partners should ask questions and make comments to find out more. Discuss your opinions about each of the stories.

▶◀ 16 To watch the video and do the activities, see the DVD ROM.

THE TEST OF TIME

SPEAKING

1 Work in groups. Discuss the questions.

- Do you like science fiction? Why? / Why not?

- Have you seen or read any of these sci-fi films or books? If yes, what did you think of them?
  - *The Time Machine*   - *Avatar*
  - *Star Wars*   - *Godzilla*
  - *The Stepford Wives*   - *Interstellar*

- Are there any famous sci-fi books or films in your language? What are they about?

- Do you think any predictions in sci-fi films have – or could – come true?

READING

2 Read the article about science-fiction films. Decide:

1 what mark out of five you think the reviewer would give for each film – and why.

2 if you agree with the reviewer's idea of what makes science fiction great.

3 According to the article, are the sentences true (T), false (F) or not mentioned (N)?

1 *Gojira* was a commercial failure.

2 The new *Godzilla* has better special effects than the first movie.

3 Countries were competing to get more nuclear weapons in the 50s.

4 People don't worry as much about nuclear weapons as they used to.

5 The Stepford wives do whatever their husbands want.

6 Joanna is killed at the end of *The Stepford Wives*.

7 There have been real stories of misuse of personal online information.

8 The writer of the article is against government control of the Internet.

4 Work in pairs. Discuss the questions.

- If you have seen any of the films mentioned, do you agree with the interpretations of them?

- Do you agree nuclear war is not a big worry these days?

- Do you agree that the stereotypes of the Stepford wives have disappeared?

- Does the Web really connect and liberate people? Is there no role for external control?

5 Complete the sentences with words from the article. The first letter of each word is given.

1 The film p_____ us to speculate about the role and limits of science.

2 The series r_____ people's attitudes towards women at the time.

3 The film a_____ the issue of old age.

4 As the plot u_____, the computer begins to take increasing control.

5 When it c_____ _____, the film created a storm.

6 Although it's around 40 years old, the film has s_____ the test of time.

7 The story r_____ with many people at the time.

8 The plot has distinct p_____ with the story of *Macbeth*.

9 The story can be seen as a m_____ for the struggle for freedom.

10 The ending leaves a number of plot strands h_____.

6 Work in groups. Discuss films, books or TV series that fit the descriptions in Exercise 5.

UNDERSTANDING VOCABULARY

Forming nouns and adjectives

There are regular ways of changing the endings of basic words when we want to change word class (noun, verb, adjective, etc.). For example, *colonial exploitation* is based on *colony* and *exploit*. However, remember that often no changes are needed.

remake the film / the **remake** wasn't very good.

7 Complete the rules with the words *nouns*, *adjectives* or *verbs*.

1 _____ based on _____ often have the following endings: *-al, -ial, -y, -ic, -ical, -less, -ful*.

2 _____ based on _____ often have the following endings: *-ive, -ative, -ed, -ing, -able, -ant*.

3 _____ based on _____ often have the following endings: *-ity, -ness, -ance, -ence*.

4 _____ based on _____ often have the following endings: *-ment, -ion, -ation, -ance*.

8 Correct the words with the wrong form in the sentences below. Don't remove or add any extra words.

1 I don't get the point of films about time travel when it's a complete impossible.

2 I hate the utter stupid of action films. They're just meaningless.

3 The technology advances made over the last 50 years are incredibly impressing.

4 The level of ignorant of science among the public is a big concern.

5 Invest in space exploring is a total waste of money!

6 There's great reluctant to take prevention measures against global warming.

7 Scientists are not sufficiently reflect about the implying of their research.

8 I'm a bit cynic about drug companies' involve in medicine research.

9 Work in groups. Discuss how far you agree with each of the statements in Exercise 8.

GODZILLA
All roar and no bite

Godzilla is high on action but fails to speak to us as great sci-fi should, says Malcolm French

Perhaps the only good thing about watching Gareth Edwards' remake of *Godzilla* is it prompted me to speculate about what really makes sci-fi great. No doubt some ambitious movie executive, hearing of the original *Godzilla's* box office success, saw the 1950s film, with its laughably unrealistic monster knocking down a model of Tokyo, and thought, 'We could do this better, make it more real, more impressive.' Of course, in terms of special effects they have, but with its super CGI and explosions that blast your senses for 90 minutes this new *Godzilla* entirely misses the point.

The original Japanese film, *Gojira*, was made in 1954 at the time of an accelerating arms race and America testing nuclear weapons over the Pacific Ocean. In the film, Godzilla was a product of these tests – a sea creature mutated by radiation and roused from the deep to attack Japan. Less than ten years after the devastation wreaked by atomic bombs over Hiroshima and Nagasaki, the film reflected the real, deep fears in Japan at the time. Edwards' *Godzilla* refers back to these origins, but the film's message simply doesn't carry the same weight. Few people these days would place nuclear war high on their list of worries for the world so it all becomes rather meaningless and merely addresses teenagers' apparently infinite desire for noise and violence.

Great sci-fi speaks to the society of the day and for that reason some films are resistant to updates. *The Stepford Wives* is another case in point. The story tells of a vibrant young professional woman, Joanna, who moves to the small suburban town of Stepford with her husband. The place is full of 'perfect-looking' women who do housework and shopping and submit to their husbands' wills. Joanna rebels against this and, with two other recently-arrived friends, sets up a women's liberation group. As the plot unfolds, we discover that the Stepford wives are in fact robots controlled by the leader of a men's social club, who threatens to kill Joanna and her feminist friends. When the film came out in the mid-70s, these tensions between the traditional image of a wife, a growing feminist movement and an oppressive male society were very real. Almost 40 years later when it was remade, these stereotypes had all but disappeared and so a chilling thriller became a lame comedy.

Still, one story that has stood the test of time is James Cameron's *Avatar*. On its release, the film's incredible 3D world created much hype, but more importantly it also resonated with the political situation of the day. The depiction of humans invading a planet to exploit its natural resources had obvious parallels with colonial exploitation and came in the midst of the Iraq War, which many saw as being motivated by a Western desire to control oil supplies.

However, *Avatar* can also be seen as a metaphor for the ongoing struggles for control of the Internet, especially in the light of recent revelations about companies exploiting private data and governments spying. The planet in *Avatar* is a living network that the natives plug into through what appear to be fibre-optic cables. In this metaphor, the violent invaders are the government, intent on disrupting the freedom of Internet users. Cameron clearly presents an unfettered world-wide Web as the ideal: the invaders are sent packing and the main human protagonist fully integrates himself with the Web by *becoming* his avatar. However, like all the best sci-fi, the film also leaves some questions hanging. How real is the online world? Does the Web really connect and liberate people? Is there no role for external control?

Unfortunately, the only question *Godzilla* left me with was: 'Has anyone got any paracetamol?'

VITAL STATISTICS

SPEAKING

1 **Work in groups. Discuss the questions.**

- Do you think you're good at using and understanding maths, data and statistics?
- What do you think are the most important uses of data and statistics?
- Do you have to use data or statistics in your work / studies? If so, to do what?
- Can you think of times in your daily life when you're exposed to statistics?

VOCABULARY Statistics

2 **Complete the sentences with these nouns.**

anomaly	ends	link
belief	evidence	research
correlation	interest	scrutiny

1 **Contrary to popular** _____, the latest statistics show crime has been falling and not getting worse, as some newspapers suggest.

2 The _____ they carried out is **fundamentally flawed**. The sample group wasn't chosen at **random** – they were **self-selected**.

3 Because **a number of variables** weren't covered by the data, it's difficult to **establish a causal** _____ **between** gaming and bad behaviour.

4 There is **conflicting** _____. Some data shows a correlation, some doesn't.

5 The data showed **a negative** _____ **between** income **and** birth rate: the richer the country, the lower the birth rate.

6 The research didn't come up with the 'right' result so the company **twisted the figures to suit its own** _____.

7 As it's the run-up to the election, the government **has a vested** _____ **in** removing people from the unemployment figures.

8 The figures **don't stand up to** _____ when you look at them closely. They're full of holes.

9 It's too early to say if these two figures are part of a new **upward trend** or whether they are **a statistical** _____.

3 **Work in pairs. Use some of the language in bold in Exercise 2 to discuss why it might be important to ask these questions about research.**

1 Who was the research commissioned by?
2 How was the data collected?
3 How big was the sample?
4 Has the research been peer reviewed?
5 Are the figures presented in their full context?
6 Does the data explain the conclusions?

I CAN GIVE YOU MY 93.4% ASSURANCE THAT THERE IS LESS THAN A 65.6% POSSIBILITY THAT THIS EXCERCISE WILL SIMPLY GENERATE 34.8% MORE MEANINGLESS STATISTICS

LISTENING

4 ▶ 22 **Listen to an extract from a radio programme about statistics. Why is each question in Exercise 3 important to consider when talking about statistics?**

5 ▶ 22 **Work in pairs. Why were the groups of numbers and statistics below mentioned? Listen again and check your ideas.**

1 60%, 2, 50% and 25%
2 50 and 5,000
3 10,000, 12,000 and 20%
4 1,000, 1,400 and 40%
5 twice and 1,600
6 50%

6 **Work in pairs. Discuss the questions.**

- Which do you think is the most important question to ask about research? Why?
- What organisations commission research? What about? Is it all equally trustworthy?
- What other correlations about what makes people healthy or ill have you heard of? Has a causal link been proved yet? Why? / Why not?
- Have you heard of any politicians using statistics that don't stand up to scrutiny?
- Have you heard of any other stories about statistics or conclusions being twisted? What happened?
- What downward and upward trends have you heard of recently? Do you know what caused them?

GRAMMAR

Passives

We use passives to focus attention on who or what an action affects. Passive verb forms use the verb *be* + past participle. However, other passive constructions are also commonly used.

7 **Work in pairs. Look at the sentences from the listening and do the following:**

1 Underline the passive constructions.
2 Decide who / what the doer of each action is.
3 See if you can write each sentence without using passives.

a *Far from doing 100% better than a rival, Company B's actually being hugely outperformed.*

b *Statistics can be used to manipulate, but they also inform policy development.*

c *Researchers may get pressured into finding positive results.*

d *A food company is having some research done to see if its product has health benefits.*

e *So next, statistics – often thought to be the worst kind of lying there is!*

f *They may worry about not being employed again, which may affect their conclusions.*

g *Obviously, research in a respected journal, reviewed by other experts, will be better than something published anonymously online.*

G Check your ideas on page 93 and do Exercise 1.

DO YOU AGREE THAT NATIONAL POLLS ARE FAIR AND UNBIASED, OR ARE YOU SOME KIND OF MORON?

©Glenn and Gary McCoy/Distributed by Universal Uclick via CartoonStock.com

8 **Complete the stories with the correct form (active or passive) of the verbs.**

1 Whenever heavy snow ¹_____ (fall), a journalist would call the headquarters of the traffic police and ask how many car crashes ²_____ (report). The news would then ³_____ (lead) with a story like: 'Two feet of snow ⁴_____ (dump) on the South today, causing huge traffic jams and 28 accidents.' One day, the journalist asked how many crashes were typical for clear sunny days. The answer? 48!

2 A study ⁵_____ (publish) in a child education journal ⁶_____ (find) that toddlers in pre-school were more aggressive than kids who ⁷_____ (keep) at home with Mum. The kids were observed over six months from their third birthday and 'aggression' ⁸_____ (define) as stealing toys, pushing other children and starting fights.

3 A small study conducted after motorcyclists ⁹_____ (force) by law to wear helmets discovered that the actual number of injuries ¹⁰_____ (treat) in hospital leapt suddenly.

4 Last year, an online magazine on ecological topics conducted a poll that ¹¹_____ (reveal) that 85% of people felt that rules around experiments ¹²_____ (conduct) on live animals ought ¹³_____ (tighten).

5 The government claimed that, as a result of their policies, the murder rate in the city ¹⁴_____ (reduce) by 30% in just eight years, falling from 130 a year at the beginning of the period to just 91 last year.

9 **Work in groups. Discuss what problems there might be with the statistics above. Think about the questions in Exercise 3.**

10 ▶ **23** **Listen and see if you were right about the problems. What lessons can be learned from each story?**

G For further practice, see Exercise 2 on page 93.

SPEAKING

11 **Work in groups. Discuss what you think each quotation about statistics means. How far do you agree with each one? Explain why.**

'There are three kinds of lies: lies, damned lies and statistics.'

'Statistics are no substitute for judgement.'

'Statistics go in one ear and out the other. We respond more to stories than numbers.'

'Statistics show that of those who contract the habit of eating, very few survive.'

'Smoking is one of the leading causes of all statistics.'

'We are all just statistics, born to consume resources.'

8

A helping hand

IN THIS UNIT YOU LEARN HOW TO:

- describe scenery and natural landscapes
- emphasise your opinions
- tell the stories behind photos
- talk about communication
- discuss stereotypes
- describe animals, their habitats and their habits

SPEAKING

1 Work in pairs. Student A: you are the photographer who took this photo. Student B: interview Student A to find out the story behind the photo and how they came to take it.

2 Change roles. The person being interviewed should now think of a different story.

3 Work in groups. Tell each other about a time when you saw an animal in the wild. Then choose the best story to tell the rest of the class.

NATURE AND NURTURE

ABSOLUTELY BREATHTAKING

VOCABULARY Describing scenery

1 Label the picture with these words.

range	plains	crater	river mouth
cliff	dunes	cove	glacier
peak	ridge	gorge	waterfall

2 Work in pairs. Decide if both or only one of the words in italics is possible.

1 It's very popular with birdwatchers because it's at the mouth of *a river* / *some dunes* and there's a lot of *wetland* / *craters* that attract birds.

2 There's a very *narrow* / *steep* ridge leading up to the main peak and the views are *breathtaking* / *stunning* – if you're not too scared to look down!

3 We sometimes gather mushrooms in the woodland near us, but you have to be careful not to *stray from* / *stick to* the paths as it's so *thick* / *dense* you can easily get lost.

4 It's miles from civilisation, really. You just drive along dirt *roads* / *tracks* across these huge *flat* / *rolling* plains. And it's all pretty *lush* / *barren* – just brown grassland.

5 It's a mecca for climbers because there are these amazing *sheer* / *jagged* cliffs on either side of the *valley* / *gorge*. I saw quite a few people climbing without ropes. They must be nuts.

6 The road winds along the coastal cliffs and there are these little coves where you can scramble down to *sandy* / *rocky* beaches and have a dip. The water's amazing – *crystal clear* / *very murky*.

3 With your partner, discuss the questions.

- Which of the features in Exercises 1 and 2 do you have in your country? Whereabouts?

- Which parts of your country do you think are the most beautiful? Which are the worst? Why? Have you been to these areas? When? Why?

- Are any parts of your country popular with these people? Why?
  birdwatchers   climbers   hunters
  cyclists   divers   campers

LISTENING

4 ▶ **24** Listen to two conversations where people are talking about photos. Answer the questions about each conversation.

1 Where were they?

2 What were they doing there?

3 What was the scenery like?

5 ▶ **24** Work in pairs. Try to remember what the speakers said about the following. Then listen again and check your ideas.

Conversation 1	Conversation 2
1 a cable car	6 a family reunion
2 a bit of a scramble	7 some creepy-crawly
3 rusty cables	8 paradise
4 a head for heights	9 jellyfish
5 a death wish	10 debt

70

6 With your partner, discuss the questions.

- Which of the two places sounds better to you? Why?
- Do you have any photos of your friends and family – or of recent holidays – on your phone? If you do, show them to your partner and talk about them.
- Would you ever do any extreme sport like base jumping? Do you know anyone who has?
- Are there any things you think you would appreciate more now than you did in the past?

DEVELOPING CONVERSATIONS

Emphatic tags

We often add tags to emphasise our opinions. We usually begin with a pronoun + *really* and we then either repeat the auxiliary if there is one or add *do / does / did* if there isn't.

A: *Wow! The view from up there must've been pretty breathtaking!*

B: *Yeah, it was stunning, **it really was**.*

7 Add emphatic tags to the sentences.

1 I wouldn't drive it if I were you.
2 The views were just stunning.
3 The scenery takes your breath away.
4 I just love it there.
5 It made no difference whatsoever.
6 He'll never change.
7 I've never been anywhere like it.
8 That sounds amazing.

8 ▶ 25 Listen and check your ideas. Then practise saying the sentences with the added tag. In the tag, stress *really*.

9 Work in pairs. How many different replies using emphatic tags can you think of for each sentence below?

1 *Oh, it was just perfect, it really was.*

Put it this way: I wouldn't recommend it, I really wouldn't.

Wonderful! I could've quite happily stayed for another week, I really could.

1 What was your hotel like? Was it OK?
2 So, was it worth climbing to the top?
3 What was your tour guide like?
4 You cycled there, didn't you?
5 It must've been nice being away from civilisation for a few days.
6 What did you think of the place?

CONVERSATION PRACTICE

10 Choose one of these tasks.

a Think of a place you have visited that had interesting scenery. Think about what you were doing there, how you travelled around and what the place was like.

b Choose two or three photos from File 18 on page 100. Imagine you took them and be ready to explain where they are, what was happening, what you were doing there and what the places were like.

11 Now work in pairs. Tell each other about your places. Try to use as much language from this lesson as you can. Your partner should ask questions and add comments while listening.

🎥 17 To watch the video and do the activities, see the DVD ROM.

NURTURE NOT NATURE

SPEAKING

1 Work in groups. Read the introduction to an article. Then discuss the questions below.

You've probably heard of the idea that men and women are so different they could be from different planets. The theory was actually popularised over 20 years ago by Dr John Gray, author of the book *Men are from Mars and Women are from Venus*, which has now sold over 50 million copies worldwide. The book suggests that relationships fail because we don't take account of the fundamentally different ways men and women communicate. His book's been followed by numerous other self-help guides over the years, many by Gray himself. There have also been other best-sellers such as Steve Harvey's *Act Like a Lady, Think Like a Man* and Sheryl Sanberg's *Lean In*, which suggests that women need to overcome their natural tendencies and be more pushy – more like men – in order to get ahead in business. But how far are these behaviours natural – hard-wired in our brains through evolution – and what role does nurture and culture have to play?

- Have you heard of any of the books mentioned? Are they the kind of thing you like to read?
- Why do you think such books are so popular?
- Which of these ideas from Gray's book do you think are true?
  - Women talk more than men.
  - Women know and use more words than men.
  - Women talk about their feelings more.
  - Men interrupt more than women.
  - Men are more competitive than women.
  - Men are more direct than women when speaking.
- Do you think these behaviours are 'hard-wired' or the result of nurture and culture? Why?

LISTENING

2 ▶ 26 Listen to a lecture about language and gender by a lecturer in linguistics. Take notes on what you hear.

3 Work in pairs. Compare your notes and check what you understood.

4 ▶ 26 With your partner, use your notes to answer the questions. Then listen again and check your answers.

1 How are the figures 20,000, 7,000, 16,000 and 45,000 connected?
2 Which of these figures are more reliable? Why?
3 What are the findings of the studies by Hyde and Chambers?
4 Why does the lecturer cite the study in Gapun?
5 What do Deborah Cameron and Simon Baron-Cohen disagree about?
6 What's the lecturer's conclusion?

5 Work in groups. Talk about note-taking. Discuss:

- whether you think you're good at taking notes or not.
- what system you use when taking notes – and why.
- when you need to take notes in your daily life.
- whether you take notes in the same way in your own language and in English.
- what you normally do with your notes after your English class / a meeting / a lecture.
- how you think you could improve your note-taking skills.

6 Look at audio script 26 on page 109. Find all the verbs and adjectives that collocate with these nouns.

research	evidence	study
myth	stereotype	claim

7 Work in groups. Discuss the questions.

- Is there anything you didn't fully understand in the lecture?
- Is there anything in the lecture that surprised you?
- Is there anything you agree or disagree with? What? To what extent?
- Do you agree that nurture is more important than nature in determining how people act? Why? / Why not?

GRAMMAR

Auxiliaries

Auxiliaries are words like *be, have, do, will, must*, etc. that we use to make negatives and questions. We also use them to avoid repetition and to add emphasis.

8 Work in pairs. Complete the sentences from the listening with the correct auxiliary verbs in the correct form. Explain why each auxiliary is being used.

1 After all, women are better communicators, _____ they?
2 Baron-Cohen's choice is simply based on the fact jobs in such fields have traditionally been occupied by women. And why _____ they?
3 When talking to a boss, we won't butt in, but they _____ .
4 Research in the journal *Science* has shown both sexes talk equally as much, and in _____ so use on average 16,000 words per day.
5 The neutrality of the situation is important. Some men _____ speak over others more, but this is not to do with gender.

G Check your ideas on page 94 and do Exercise 1.

9 Write responses to these sentences in different ways using auxiliaries.

1 *Have you? What did you think of it?*

Yeah. It's rubbish, isn't it?

1 I've actually read *Men are from Mars*.

2 I don't think you can just totally dismiss stereotypes.

3 I'd love to live on a tropical island.

4 I wasn't allowed to play with dolls when I was a kid.

5 I don't have much of a head for heights.

6 I find baking quite fascinating, as weird as that may sound.

10 Work in pairs. Take turns to say the sentences from Exercise 9. Your partner should reply. Continue each conversation for as long as possible.

11 Work with a new partner. Find six things you have in common and four you don't. Then report back your results to the class. How many different auxiliaries can you use?

My partner would like to do a Master's degree sometime, and I would too. She's thinking of going to Australia to study, though, whereas I'm not. I'd rather stay here. She's really into movies, and so am I, but she likes weird arty stuff. I don't. I'm more of a big Hollywood-blockbuster-type person.

G For further practice, see Exercises 2 and 3 on page 94.

VOCABULARY Communicating

12 Complete the sentences with these pairs of words.

articulate + struggle	bush + point
manners + butting into	mince + blunt
gossip + rumours	twisting + words
listener + shoulder	shuts up + word

1 He's a terrible _____ – he's always spreading _____ about everyone in the office.

2 She's never less than 100% honest. She certainly doesn't _____ her words. She can be very _____ sometimes.

3 Once he starts talking, he never _____. No-one else can get a _____ in edgeways!

4 She's always _____ what I say and trying to put _____ into my mouth.

5 He's got no _____! He's always _____ other people's conversations.

6 She's a great _____ – always good to go to if you need a _____ to cry on.

7 He's not very _____. I mean, he seems to find it quite a _____ to express himself.

8 I wish she'd stop beating about the _____ and get to the _____. This is taking forever!

13 Work in groups. Discuss the questions.

- Do any of the sentences in Exercise 12 remind you of people you know? In what way?

- Which do you think describe you?

SPEAKING

14 Work in groups. Discuss the questions.

- Do you know any men / women who completely defy traditional gender stereotypes?

- Do you know any men / women who completely conform to gender stereotypes? In what way?

- Do you know people who are very different to the stereotype that exists of them (age, gender, nationality, etc.)?

- What stereotypes do you think other people might think you fit in with? To what degree do you think you conform to these stereotypes?

- Why do you think people stereotype others? Do you think it's useful in any way? What harm might it cause?

THE ANIMAL KINGDOM

VOCABULARY Animals

1 Work in pairs. Look at the photos and for each animal discuss:

- where you think it lives – in what kind of landscape and in what part of the world. Explain why.
- why it might have adapted as it has and what special features it might have developed.
- what you think it might eat. Explain why.

2 Find examples in the photos of these things.

hoof	legs	nostrils	horn	toe
scales	fur	claw	teeth	hump
tail	feelers	beak	wing	breast

3 Match the two parts of the sentences.

1	It builds	a	through tree bark.
2	It can sense	b	a high-pitched squeal.
3	It tunnels	c	reserves of fat.
4	It can blend	d	its chest.
5	It can withstand	e	a nest.
6	It gnaws	f	into the background.
7	It puffs up	g	the slightest movement.
8	It leaps out	h	and snatches its prey.
9	It stores	i	freezing temperatures.
10	It lets out	j	down into the earth.

4 Work in pairs. Think of an animal for each of the sentences in Exercise 3. Discuss why each action might be done.

5 ▶ 27 Listen to two short descriptions of animals. Find out:

1 which animals in the photos are being described.

2 what parts of the body are mentioned and what they are used for.

UNDERSTANDING VOCABULARY

Compound adjectives

Compound adjectives are made up of two or more words. We put a hyphen between these words. Compound adjectives are often formed using noun + adjective (*water-resistant*); adjective + noun (*last-minute*); adjective, adverb or noun + present / past participle (*good-looking, densely-populated, long-lasting*) or number + noun (*a ten-minute walk*).

6 Work in pairs. Think of one noun that each of these adjectives could describe.

water-resistant	star-shaped	award-winning
long-term	child-friendly	self-help
high-powered	six-lane	life-threatening
tailor-made		

7 Work in pairs. You have five minutes to come up with as many different compound adjective + noun collocations as you can, using the adjectives from Exercise 6. You can change either word of the compound adjectives to make new ones.

an Oscar-winning film   an award-worthy innovation

READING

8 Work in groups of four: two As and two Bs. You are going to read about another animal in the photos.

Student As: read the text on this page.

Student Bs: read the text in File 19 on page 99.

Find out about:

1 the animal's habitat.

2 its behaviour.

3 its unique physical features.

4 any threats it's facing.

5 conservation efforts being made to protect it.

9 With the person who read the same text, do the following:

1 Compare what you understood about the animal – its habitat and habits and the threats it faces.

2 Decide what you feel is the most interesting fact about the animal.

3 Check you understand the phrases in bold and try to remember them.

10 Now work in new pairs: one Student A and one Student B. Close your books. Tell each other as much as you can about the animal you read about using some of the phrases in bold from the text, then do the following:

1 Discuss which animal you feel is the most interesting – and why.

2 Discuss which animal you think has the bleaker future – and why.

3 Learn at least two new useful phrases from your partner.

11 With the same partner, decide if the sentences refer to one or other of the animals – or both. Then look back at the texts and check your answers.

1 The area it traditionally lives in is shrinking.

2 It travels extensively in order to find food.

3 It may have to cope with severe food shortages.

4 It's sometimes the victim of superstitious fears.

5 It's sometimes killed for the benefit of other animals.

6 The way it performs some of its unique abilities remains a mystery.

7 It's developed an extremely unusual way of finding food.

8 Efforts are being made to increase the population.

9 It's a relatively communal creature.

10 Its mating habits can have life-threatening consequences.

SHIPS OF THE GOBI DESERT

The wild Bactrian camel is found in the Gobi desert of Mongolia and China, which ranges from boiling sand dunes to frozen hills and mountains. It has evolved to withstand the extremes of heat and cold as well as the arid landscape. It has thick eyelashes that close to **form a protective barrier** against sandstorms and it can also completely close its thin, slit-like nostrils to prevent dust entering. It eats snow in the winter months and, unlike any other camel, can also drink salt water. It is still unknown how it processes the salt water.

Excess water is stored not in its humps but in the bloodstream. The humps are largely made up of fat. The camel **draws upon these fat reserves** in times of drought and famine. Like other camels, it reduces water loss by hardly sweating or urinating. It also has a remarkably tough tongue, capable of eating **the sharp thorns of desert shrubs**. These camels are incredibly resistant to disease, which may surprise people considering their numbers are dwindling.

The wild Bactrian camels **roam widely in small herds** of two to fifteen members and will travel vast distances in search of food and water. However, they are **threatened from a number of angles**. They were heavily hunted in previous years and continue to be so where there is competition for water sources from domestic herds. They have also suffered poisoning as a result of the use of dangerous chemicals in **illegal mining activities**. Finally, they often interbreed with domestic Bactrians, which leads them to lose the capability to drink salt water.

Despite efforts to **crack down** on illegal mining and hunting, the wild Bactrian camel has become one of the rarest mammals in the world. There are now **captive breeding programmes** aimed at restoring populations.

SPEAKING

12 Choose two of the topics below to talk about. Spend a few minutes researching and preparing what you want to say about each one. Then work in groups and share your ideas.

- how much (or how little!) we should spend on animal welfare – and why

- a remarkable animal

- an animal that's a national symbol or that's culturally important

- what I remember about the animals I studied at school

- two endangered animals – and what can be done to protect them

VIDEO 4

BABY MATH

1 **Work in groups. Look at the photo and discuss the questions.**

- What is happening?
- Do you think it's a good idea to do this in this way? Why? / Why not?
- Discuss whether you think each of the following is good for babies. Explain your ideas.
  - being allowed to eat whenever they want
  - having classical music played to them
  - sleeping away from their parents
  - being made to sit up as soon as they can
  - not talking to them until they're ready to talk

2 📹 **18** **Watch the first part of a video about what knowledge babies are born with (0.00–1.44). How are the words below connected to babies' instincts and abilities – and how are some of these instincts related to other animals?**

1 submerge
2 suck
3 grasp
4 startle
5 steps

3 **Work in pairs. Discuss the questions.**

- How do you think babies' mathematical ability might be tested?
- What problems might there be when researching this ability?
- What results do you think have been found?

4 📹 **18** **Watch the second part of the video (1.45–4.15) and answer the questions in Exercise 3.**

5 **Work in pairs. Check you understand the words and phrases in bold. Then discuss what the words in italics refer to.**

1 *It* arrives with a set of **reflexes** to help it survive.

2 *It* will **intuitively** hold its breath.
3 Perhaps *this* may be the **trace** of an **ancestral** instinct for holding onto a mother's back.
4 One popular notion is that *it* starts out in the world with a completely **blank slate** mind.
5 *It* has no expectations and finds the world this incredibly confusing, chaotic **barrage** of impressions and sensations.
6 *It* seems surprised and stares at *this* **outcome** much longer.
7 *They* are **pretty consistent** and suggest that babies as young as four months can add up.
8 *They* can judge *this* with just a simple **glance**.

6 **Work in groups. Discuss how far you agree with each of the statements below. Explain your ideas.**

1 The research methods used in the video don't prove anything.
2 Kids could achieve so much more if only we pushed them a bit harder.
3 We are basically no different to most other animals.
4 Using babies in experiments is just totally unacceptable.
5 Mathematical ability is at the heart of human intelligence.

UNDERSTANDING FAST SPEECH

7 📹 **19** **Listen to an extract from the video said at natural pace. Try to write down what you hear. Then compare your ideas with a partner.**

8 📹 **20** **Try again. This time you will hear a slower version of the extract.**

9 **Check your ideas in File 10 on page 98. Groups of words are marked with / and pauses are marked //. Stressed sounds are in CAPITALS. Practise saying the extract.**

REVIEW 4

GRAMMAR AND UNDERSTANDING
VOCABULARY

1 Complete the text with one word in each space.

Stuck in my dull office job, I often used to dream of [1]_____ transported to a tropical island. It's not an uncommon thought, [2]_____ it? But then I was actually [3]_____ the opportunity to fulfil that dream when I took part in an award-[4]_____ TV programme where a group of people [5]_____ abandoned on a remote Pacific island to see how well they can survive. The island was beautiful, it really [6]_____, but we quickly discovered its downsides. Only an hour after [7]_____ dropped off, we had all [8]_____ bitten by various insects, seen snakes and [9]_____ lost in the dense jungle. I also suffered from severe dehydration, which can be [10]_____-threatening if left untreated. But I [11]_____ survive for the full four weeks of the programme and in [12]_____ so changed my outlook on life dramatically. I am so much more appreciative of what I have now than I used to [13]_____ before the programme, I really [14]_____.

2 Complete the second sentence so that it has a similar meaning to the first sentence using the word given. Do not change the word given. You must use between four and five words, including the word given.

1 I can't believe how stupid the government has been.
It's difficult to believe _____ the government's actions. **SHEER**

2 They are conducting the research for a cancer charity.
The research _____ on behalf of a cancer charity. **CARRIED**

3 I can understand why they're reluctant to help.
I think their _____. **IS**

4 We've won several prizes for the site because it's easy for children to use.
Our _____ several prizes. **AWARDED**

5 We know that the drug can help patients with heart disease.
The drug _____ in treating heart disease. **BE**

3 Complete the sentences. Use the word in brackets to form a word that fits in the space. Sometimes you need to make a compound adjective.

1 In updating the site we have created greater _____. (interact)

2 We will only find out in the _____ of time. (full)

3 The _____ nose enables the mole to find its way in the dark. (star)

4 We should be very concerned about the ongoing _____ of species. (appear)

5 It's easy to get downhearted at the _____ of the situation. (hope)

6 The animals are now bred in _____ because they are nearing _____ in the wild. (captive, extinct)

7 The breakthrough should lead to the production of more _____ _____ fabrics. (breathe, water)

VOCABULARY

4 Decide which of these nouns are parts of animals and which are connected to landscape.

claw	crater	cliff	scales	horn
hoof	cove	range	beak	jungle
fur	peak	hump	ridge	gorge

5 Match the verbs (1–10) with the collocates (a–j).

1 devise	a us to speculate / fears
2 insert	b my hand / its prey
3 reflect	c a way / a mechanism
4 prompt	d attitudes / the times
5 store	e a probe / the USB
6 snatch	f tiny movements / danger
7 sense	g the procedure / the analysis
8 address	h reserves / information
9 withstand	i the extreme cold / pressure
10 undertake	j underlying causes / the issue

6 Complete the sentences with a preposition in each space.

1 Contrary _____ popular belief, high-fat diets may not lead to heart disease.

2 The sample group was chosen _____ random.

3 Because of the small sample, several variables weren't covered _____ the data.

4 We all have a vested interest _____ the project being a success.

5 Attitudes _____ women have changed a lot since the 60s.

6 Honestly, I can never get a word _____ edgeways with him.

7 Remember, I'm always a shoulder to cry _____ if you need it.

8 Stop beating _____ the bush and get _____ the point.

9 I'm happy to take a back seat and blend _____ the background.

7 Complete the text with one word in each space. The first letters are given.

There has been an [1]up_____ trend in levels of obesity and the blame has generally been placed on saturated fat. Despite [2]co_____ evidence over the years, the most [3]pr_____ medical advice has been to reduce fats in our diet. However, a recent paper by Zoe Harcombe and James DiNicolantonio, which analysed the [4]fi_____ of hundreds of other studies in the [5]fi_____, has suggested this advice is [6]fl_____ and that there is no [7]co_____ between fat and heart disease. The researchers have themselves been criticised by some who suggest their figures don't [8]s_____ u_____ to scrutiny and the results are [9]d_____ to a failure to take into account all the [10]va_____ involved. While debate on fat is unlikely to end with Harcome and DiNocolantonio's study, many health experts have discovered sugars are strongly [11]li_____ to obesity, which is [12]pa_____ the way for new taxes being imposed on sugar in some countries.

SPEAKING

1 **Work in pairs. Look at the table and chart and discuss the questions.**
- What are the main facts, predictions and trends that the table and chart show?
- What do you think is meant by 'developed' and 'developing' countries?
- Why do you think these trends are happening?
- Can you see similar trends in your country?
- How do you feel about these changes? What is good / bad about them?

World's biggest cities by population
(in millions)

2014			2030		
1	Tokyo (Japan)	37.8	1	Tokyo (Japan)	37.2
2	Delhi (India)	25.0	2	Delhi (India)	36.1
3	Shanghai (China)	23.0	3	Shanghai (China)	30.8
4	Mexico City (Mexico)	20.8	4	Mumbai (India)	27.8
5	São Paulo (Brazil)	20.8	5	Beijing (China)	27.7
6	Mumbai (India)	20.7	6	Dhaka (Bangladesh)	27.4
7	Osaka (Japan)	20.1	7	Karachi (Pakistan)	24.8
8	Beijing (China)	19.5	8	Cairo (Egypt)	24.5
9	New York (USA)	18.6	9	Lagos (Nigeria)	24.2
10	Cairo (Egypt)	18.4	10	Mexico City (Mexico)	23.9
11	Dhaka (Bangladesh)	17.0	11	São Paulo (Brazil)	23.4
12	Karachi (Pakistan)	16.1	12	Kinshasa (Democratic Republic of Congo)	20.0

city located on coast or major river

World rural and urban populations

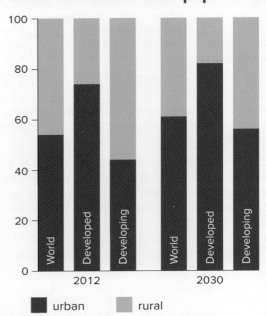

■ urban   ■ rural

WRITING

2 **Read the description of the data in the table and the chart. Find six factual mistakes.**

The table shows the 12 largest cities in the world by area in 2014 and projected figures for 2030. As can be seen, with the exception of Tokyo, all of the five main cities are predicted to grow, which is unsurprising given the continued shift from urban to rural living illustrated in the chart. In the developed world, two out of every three people already live in cities, and between now and 2030, the global urban population is expected to rise by 25%, the bulk of which will occur in developing countries. This shift towards growth in developing regions is reflected in the table. It shows that the populations of cities such as Delhi, Shanghai and Mumbai will all increase quite substantially and by 2030, African cities (Lagos and Kinshasa) are forecast to have entered the top 12 for the first time. Perhaps most remarkably, the population of Dhaka in Bangladesh looks set to increase by almost 90%. It is interesting to note that a significant minority of the cities predicted to grow are located on the coast or on major rivers, reflecting the importance of trade in urban development.

3 **Work in pairs and do the following:**
1 Compare the mistakes you found and correct them.
2 Decide one other feature of the table and chart you would draw attention to.

VOCABULARY Describing percentages

4 **Replace the words in italics with these words and phrases.**

a tiny percentage	four out of five
the vast majority	almost a fifth
a significant minority	more than halved
slightly higher	fourfold

1 The chart shows there were around 20,000 immigrants, *93%* of whom came from other European countries.

2 The graph illustrates that urban sprawl increased by *19%* over this period.

3 As is illustrated in figure 1, violent crime *fell from 5% to 2%*, while burglary rates increased *from 1.5% to 6%*.

4 As can be seen in the pie chart, *80% of* customers were satisfied with the service, which was *6% more* than last year.

5 This is illustrated in figure 3, which shows that only *0.1%* of household income is spent on books.

6 The survey indicated that *43%* of respondents were concerned about the effects of the proposals.

GRAMMAR

Describing changes

In academic writing and journalism, passive constructions are often used instead of *be going to* or *will* to describe future predictions.

All the main cities **are predicted to** *grow.*

Between now and 2030, the global urban population **is expected to** *rise by 25%.*

New York and Osaka, meanwhile, **are projected to** *drop out of the top 12 altogether.*

We can use a perfect infinitive to show we think something will happen before a point in the future.

By 2030, *African cities ...* **are forecast to have entered** the top 12 for the first time.

5 Rewrite the sentences using the verbs in brackets.

1 By 2025, the population will have risen to 15 million. (project)

2 In the next 20 years, the rural population will start falling. (predict)

3 African cities will grow rapidly over the next few years. (expect)

4 China will become the world's largest economy in the next ten years. (forecast)

Remember that we use other tenses to describe past and present trends.

Between 2000 and 2005, Internet usage **rose** *dramatically.*

Since 2000, overall crime **has fallen** *steadily.*

The number of bilingual schools **is** *currently* **increasing**.

See also the Grammar reference on page 86 (perfect forms).

---

6 Work in pairs. Think of an example for each of the following. Discuss why they are happening / have happened and predict how they will develop in the future.

1 an upward trend

2 a downward trend

3 a general shift from one thing to another

KEY WORDS FOR WRITING

of whom / of which

We can give information about a part of a group or statistic we have just mentioned using *of whom* or *of which*. *Of whom* refers to people and *of which* to things. We modify these with *all*, *some*, *many*, *the vast majority*, etc. to show the proportion of the group we are talking about.

The global urban population is expected to rise by 25%, **the bulk of which** *will occur in developing countries.*

There were around 20,000 immigrants, **91% of whom** *came from other European countries.*

7 Rewrite each pair of sentences as one sentence using *of whom* or *of which*.

1 The government donates 0.6% of GDP as aid. The bulk of that money goes to countries in Africa.

2 There were 2,650 fatalities from car accidents last year. The vast majority of the accidents were caused by driver error.

3 The city has around 200,000 inhabitants. This figure includes 25,000 students.

4 There was a significant fall in crime in the last decade. A large part of the drop was attributed to rising living standards.

5 The survey interviewed 950 people altogether. The interviewees were mostly 18 to 25 years old.

PRACTICE

8 Work in pairs. Look at the visuals below and discuss the following:

- what the pie chart and graph generally show
- the main facts, trends and predictions
- key statistics that illustrate the trend
- any surprising aspects you would highlight

9 Write a description of the main trends illustrated in the chart and graph. Use between 150 and 200 words.

Fig.1 Website content languages

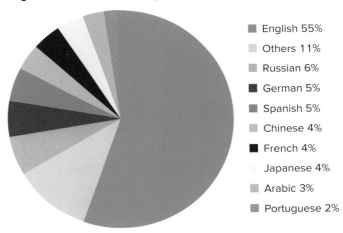

- English 55%
- Others 11%
- Russian 6%
- German 5%
- Spanish 5%
- Chinese 4%
- French 4%
- Japanese 4%
- Arabic 3%
- Portuguese 2%

Source: w3techs.com

Fig.2 Millions of adults learning English

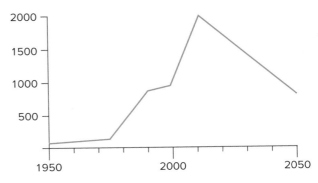

Source: The English Company

2 WRITING Building an argument

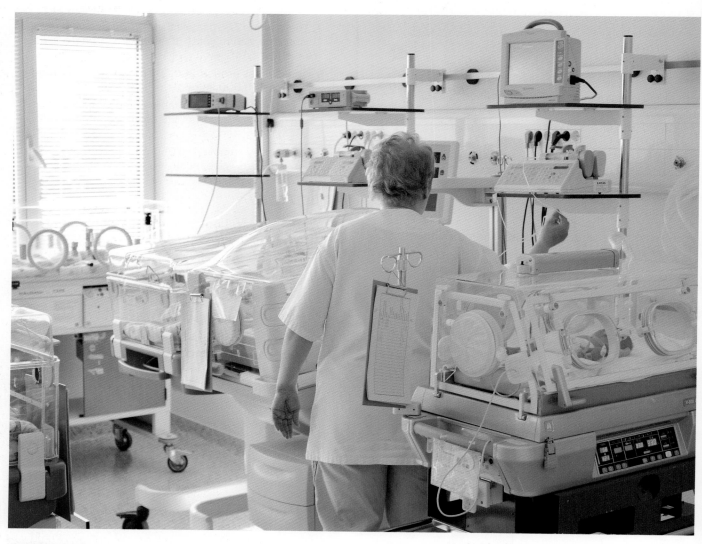

SPEAKING

1 Work in groups. Discuss these questions.

- Do you know anyone who works in health care? Who? What do they do? Do they enjoy it?
- How is health care funded in your country – through taxation, insurance or direct payments?
- What are the strengths and weaknesses of the health care system in your country?
- If you could change one thing about the system, what would it be? Why?

WRITING

2 You are going to read an introduction to an essay with the title below. Before you read, work in pairs and discuss the questions.

'The government should provide free health care for all.'

Discuss.

1 What makes the essay title relevant these days?

2 What are the main issues that need to be addressed in the essay?

3 What else might be included in the introduction?

3 Read the introduction and see if it covers the same things you thought of in Exercise 2.

'THE GOVERNMENT SHOULD PROVIDE FREE HEALTH CARE FOR ALL.' DISCUSS.

The health of a nation is clearly of paramount importance and measures of health and life expectancy are seen as key indicators of a country's success. Given this, some argue that health care provision is the government's responsibility and should be free for all. However, there are several points here that need addressing. Firstly, what do we mean by free? Secondly, *what* health care is to be 'free'? And, finally, what is the government's role? In this essay, I will argue that 'free for all' is an impossibility and that while a basic level of provision should be totally free to *a few*, the government's role in health care should be minimal.

4 With your partner, answer the questions.

1 What arguments do you think will be given to back up the writer's opinion?

2 How do you think the information in the essay will be organised?

5 Read the rest of the essay opposite and check your ideas from Exercise 4.

6 Complete the essay with these words.

| as such | furthermore | indeed | otherwise | such |
| firstly | however | in short | secondly | while |

The cost of health care is not 'free'. ¹_____, in many countries, costs are spiralling. Health care must be paid for either via taxation, through insurance premiums or by direct payments to doctors and ²_____ it is impossible for it to be free for *all*. The issue is, therefore, whether *some* people should be exempt from paying. I would argue that taxation should be limited to providing preventative health measures, such as vaccinations and hospital treatment in life-threatening emergencies, for those too poor to have health insurance. As well as maintaining social cohesion, ³_____ measures prevent the spread of diseases that threaten the whole of society and they also benefit everyone economically. However, some would claim there are economic and individual benefits to be gained from more health care intervention. They point to cancer treatments to extend life, operations that restore eyesight or therapy for depression. ⁴_____ this is largely true, in a 'free for all' system these individual claims compete for the limited funding that is available. Each individual sees their treatment as essential, but surely they are impossible to compare in terms of value to society. ⁵_____, would you trust the government to decide? Insurance-based systems, ⁶_____, do not have this problem. ⁷_____, insurance means money is spent by individuals on the treatment they personally need. ⁸_____, insurance companies provide an incentive to reduce risky behaviours such as smoking by charging higher premiums. In a 'free for all' system the effects of these antisocial behaviours are also *paid for* by all. ⁹_____ then, the government should provide free basic health care for a few through taxation, but ¹⁰_____ its role should be restricted to setting the legal framework for an insurance-based health system. This is better and fairer for all.

7 Work in pairs. Discuss the questions.

- How would you divide the text into paragraphs?
- Do you think the essay is otherwise clear and well organised? Why? / Why not?
- How does the writer indicate to the reader the arguments he / she finds weak?
- To what degree does the writer's opinion reflect your own? Where do you agree / disagree? Why?

KEY WORDS FOR WRITING

indeed

Indeed can be used:

1 to introduce a sentence that exemplifies or expands on a previously made point.
*The cost of health care is not 'free'. **Indeed**, in many countries, costs are spiralling.*

2 for emphasis after *very* + adjective / adverb.
*The cost of health care in the US is very high **indeed**.*

3 to emphasise that something there was some doubt about is actually true.
*Despite the hospital's denial, statistics showed that the hospital was **indeed** underperforming.*

8 Add *indeed* in the correct place in the sentences. There are two examples of each of the uses in the box.

1 After much questioning, he was eventually forced to admit that there was something wrong.

2 There are those in society who do not pay sufficient attention to their own health. Many actively abuse it.

3 Following repeated accusations, it was later proven that the test results had been falsified.

4 The final results of the experiment were very strange.

5 Putting such a theory into practice would be hard. You might say almost impossible.

6 Cultural identities in any society vary so widely as to make the extraction of common features very difficult.

9 Write sentences to exemplify or expand on the sentences below.

1 The government simply cannot afford to expand health care any further. Indeed, …

2 Governments can always find money to fund things when it suits them. Indeed, …

3 Every election brings new pledges to increase spending on the health service. Indeed, …

4 In countries where free health care for all is the norm, the system does not always function as well as we might imagine. Indeed, …

10 Work in pairs and compare your ideas. Who wrote better follow-up sentences?

PRACTICE

11 Work in pairs. Discuss possible reasons why people might agree or disagree with each of the following statements and then discuss your own opinions.

1 'Nuclear energy is the most realistic long-term option we have.' Discuss.

2 'Rather than bringing countries closer together, globalisation has led to increased nationalism.' Discuss.

3 'There should be a maximum working week for all of 35 hours.' How far do you agree?

12 Write short introductions for each of the three essay titles, using the ideas and model in Exercises 2 and 3.

13 Compare your introductions with a partner. Can you see any ways in which your partner's work could be improved?

14 Write an essay of around 300 words in response to one of the titles in Exercise 11. You should aim for five paragraphs. Try to use *indeed* at least once.

3 WRITING Reviews

SPEAKING

1 **Work in groups. Discuss the questions.**

- How often do you do the things below? Are there any things you never do? Why not?
- Can you remember the last time you did each activity? What was it like?

see plays at the theatre	read novels
go to exhibitions	go to the ballet
go to small gigs	go to big concerts
see films at the cinema	go to the opera
see musicals	read poetry

VOCABULARY Reviews

2 **Complete the sentences with these pairs of words.**

abstract + sculptures	production + plot
album + encores	rhyme + collection
based + set	sets + choreography
orchestration + role	symphony + finale
prose + multi-layered	technique + partner

1 _____ on a true story and _____ in 1940s Texas, the new release by director Jackie Lee tackles issues of violence and sexism that remain highly relevant today.

2 Generally avoiding such conventions as _____ and punctuation, this _____ contains some wonderful, albeit challenging, pieces of poetry.

3 Opening with the fan favourite *Poverty Train*, the group then powered through the bulk of their latest _____ and ended up returning for two _____ packed with crowd-pleasers.

4 The _____ are amazing, the songs wonderful and the _____ is just out of this world.

5 Featuring both figurative and _____ work, this collection spans five decades of Morton's life and also features some of her rarely seen _____.

6 This is the fourth _____ of this classic that I've seen and it's undoubtedly the best. The cast are excellent and the _____ gripping from start to finish.

7 Dorothy Gilbert's powerful _____ allows her to both carve the most beautiful shapes and move gently through them, while newcomer Andrei Agapov is surely her ideal _____.

8 Despite the sparkling, imaginative _____, there were so many twists and turns that at times the _____ plot was nearly impossible to follow.

9 With its colourful, rich _____ and with tenor Richard Hamilton making his debut in the leading _____, this staging is one of the season's must-sees.

10 Whilst not my favourite _____, the orchestra's performance was nevertheless gripping and the grand _____ even brought tears to my eyes.

3 **Match the sentences in Exercise 2 to the ten activities in Exercise 1.**

4 **Choose at least six words from Exercise 2 that describe things you've seen or read. Then work in pairs and tell your partner as much as you can about each thing.**

WRITING

5 **Read the review of a British musical. Then work in pairs and discuss the questions.**

- How many stars out of five do you think the reviewer gave the musical? Why?
- Does *Billy Elliot* sound like the kind of thing you'd enjoy? Why? / Why not?
- What do you learn about the plot? Does it remind you of any other films / books, etc.?
- What's the function of each of the five paragraphs?

ABOUT	REVIEWS	COMMENTS	NEWS	PHOTOS

BILLY ELLIOT

Given that it has been adapted from the film of the same name, it is no surprise that the musical version of *Billy Elliot* is full of cinematic suspense. Set against the backdrop of the miners' strike in 1980s Britain, the plot revolves around a young boy who rejects his father's moves to push him into boxing in favour of ballet lessons, a decision which initially causes conflict in his family but which eventually leads him to fame and fortune.

The beautifully choreographed drama unfolds in a tense, gripping manner and the stage is exploited to the full. The scenes that alternate between Billy's ballet lessons and his father's battles against the police on the picket lines at the mine are particularly powerful. The sets are incredibly evocative and capture the mood of social unrest excellently, transporting the audience to another time and place.

When one stops to consider the extreme youth of its main star – Nat Sweeney, who plays Billy, is only twelve years old – the show becomes even more remarkable. Nat is dazzling and I found myself unable to take my eyes off him for the whole performance. He brings a vulnerability and tenderness to the role that left many in tears.

If I do have a criticism, then I suppose it would be the music, written by pop legend Sir Elton John. Whilst it is often uplifting and anthemic, it does start to feel somewhat formulaic after a time. Therein lies the other slight problem – at just over three hours, the show is perhaps 30 minutes too long. By the time the excellent cast had received three standing ovations, I'd been in my seat for almost 200 minutes!

Regardless of these minor flaws, this is nevertheless an outstanding spectacle and a must-see for anyone keen on contemporary musicals.

KEY WORDS FOR WRITING

given and nevertheless

Given means 'considering'. It shows you are taking account of a fact when you give an opinion.

Given *that it has been adapted from the film, it is no surprise that the musical version of* Billy Elliot *is full of cinematic suspense.*

Nevertheless is used with *despite, while, regardless,* etc. to emphasise that something is true despite what you first said. It is also used like *however* to refer back to a previous sentence.

Regardless of these minor flaws, this is **nevertheless** *an outstanding spectacle.*

The film lasts four hours. **Nevertheless,** *the time flies by.*

6 **Match the two parts of the sentences.**

1 The play received very poor reviews,
2 The play was a remarkable success,
3 Given that the concert was quite short and the band refused to give an encore,
4 Irrespective of the band's refusal to give an encore,
5 While Watson only plays a minor role in the film,
6 Given that Watson only plays a minor role,

a she nevertheless outshines everyone with her remarkable performance.
b but nevertheless went on to be hugely popular.
c it's remarkable that she won an Oscar.
d given how low expectations surrounding it were.
e it was nevertheless an amazing concert.
f it was unsurprising there were boos and complaints as the audience left the auditorium.

7 **Work in pairs. Think of three different ways to complete each of the sentences below.**

1 While her recent collection has been badly received by the press, I nevertheless found it ...
2 Despite a huge budget, the film nevertheless ...
3 Given the length of the novel, ...
4 This is a very young orchestra. Nevertheless, ...

PRACTICE

8 **Write a review of a concert, album, exhibition, ballet, musical or novel. Use between 250 and 300 words and try to use as much language from this lesson as you can.**

4 WRITING Describing processes

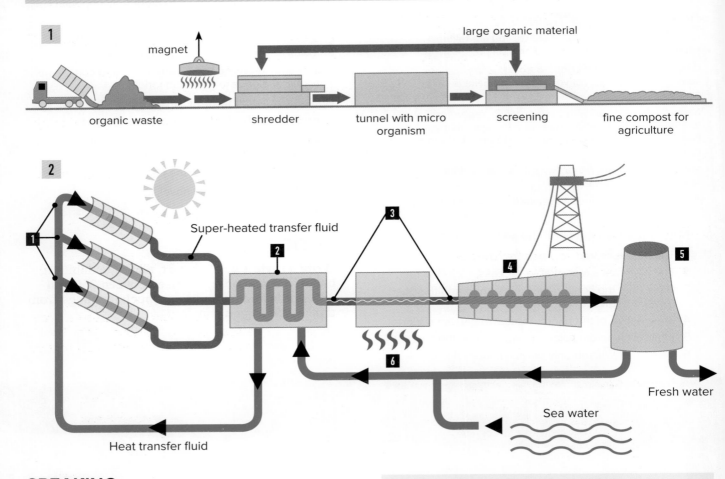

1 magnet — large organic material

organic waste — shredder — tunnel with micro organism — screening — fine compost for agriculture

2 Super-heated transfer fluid

Heat transfer fluid — Sea water — Fresh water

SPEAKING

1 Work in groups. Discuss the questions:

- What is involved in the following processes? Have you ever been involved in any of them?
  - a visa application
  - getting a non-emergency operation
  - buying and selling online
  - publishing a book or making a film
  - a criminal court case
  - getting compensation for something
  - getting rid of your rubbish
  - providing electricity or tap water

- Have you ever experienced a difficult bureaucratic / legal process? What happened?

- Do you think it's important to know about how we get consumer products and services? Why? / Why not? Are there any product or service processes you'd like to know more about?

WRITING

2 Work in pairs. Look at the two diagrams above. Discuss what processes you think they show and what you think might happen in each case.

3 Now read the text that describes Figure 2 and label 1–6 in the diagram.

4 Complete the description with these linkers.

| meanwhile | whereby | thus | which | as |

The diagram shows a process known as Concentrating Solar Power (CSP) [1]_____ solar energy is used to create steam to power electrical generators.

Large parabolic troughs are directed at the sun. The mirrored surfaces of the troughs reflect the sun's rays and concentrate them onto pipes carrying a fluid that is [2]_____ heated up to a very high temperature. This super-heated fluid passes through a heat exchanger, where it boils water and creates steam, before returning in a loop back to the parabolic trough. The steam [3]_____ is conveyed through pipes at high pressure to a generator, where it drives turbines to create electricity. [4]_____ the steam goes through the turbine it loses heat and is then further cooled in a tower, converting it back into water. The water then continues in a loop back to the heat exchanger, where it is again boiled to create steam. In the absence of sunshine, the steam is generated by supplementary gas-powered heaters.

CSP offers a number of benefits: it provides clean sustainable energy; it can make use of large tracts of unused desert land; and it can be adapted to make use of sea water, [5]_____ can be easily desalinated at the cooling-tower stage, thereby providing much-needed fresh water in arid zones.

5 What is the purpose of the three paragraphs? How does the writer avoid using personal pronouns (*I, we, me, us,* etc.) in the text? Would you avoid such pronouns in similar texts in your language?

SPEAKING

6 Work in pairs. Discuss the questions.

- Do you think the process you read about would be a good idea in your country? Why? / Why not?
- What benefits / problems are there with the following energy sources or energy-saving schemes? Do you have any of them in your country? Is there any opposition to them?
  - wind farms
  - fracking
  - solar farms
  - subsidies for renewable energies
  - oil / gas drilling
  - nuclear power plants
  - hydroelectric dams
  - subsidies for improving insulation

VOCABULARY Processes

7 Replace the words in italics with these words and rewrite each sentence in the passive.

insulate	categorise	assemble
screen	discard	ship
break down	box	power
remove	proofread	select

1 They *take out* plastic from the rubbish manually.
2 They *wrap* the pipes with foam to minimise heat loss.
3 They *check* the final product for impurities.
4 They *sort* the tea leaves into different grades according to size and quality.
5 They don't *throw away* anything during the process to maximise efficiency.
6 They *choose* potential jury members randomly from the electoral roll.
7 They *put together* the parts in a central plant.
8 They *check* the final manuscript for spelling mistakes and other errors.
9 They *package* the oranges and load them onto lorries.
10 They *drive* the turbines by forcing water through them.
11 They use microbes to *decompose* the oil into droplets.
12 They only take payment after they *send* the order from the warehouse.

8 Work in pairs. Discuss the questions.

- What processes do you think each of the sentences in Exercise 7 are part of?
- Why might different processes use these things?

a filter	a conveyor belt	a pump
a magnet	a furnace	an algorithm

KEY WORDS FOR WRITING

whereby, thereby and *thus*

Whereby explains the way something is done according to a method, agreement, rule, etc.

Thereby and *thus* both show the result of a particular process previously mentioned.

9 Complete the sentences with *whereby* or *thereby*.

1 Glassblowing is the process _____ glass is heated and then shaped.
2 The milk is heated to around 70%, _____ killing the vast majority of microbes.
3 We have to comply with strict regulations _____ our machines are inspected weekly, _____ ensuring total safety.
4 There's a trade-in scheme _____ any car over fifteen years old can be scrapped for $3,000 when buying a new car.

10 Work in groups. How many of these natural, industrial and legal rules and processes can you explain in one sentence with *whereby*? For how many can you add a possible result using *thus* or *thereby*?

desalination	Gaia
hydroelectric power	metamorphosis
a veto	photosynthesis
osmosis	auditing
distillation	landfill
an embargo	a high court appeal

PRACTICE

11 Choose either the diagram of the composting process (Figure 1) or draw a diagram to represent a process you discussed in Exercise 1 or 8.

12 Write a description of the process. Use between 150 and 200 words.

Archimede Solar Energy Power Plant,
Perugia, Italy

GRAMMAR REFERENCE

1 CITIES

PERFECT FORMS

Present perfect simple

The present perfect simple shows that something happened or started before now. There is usually a present result.

*The Guggenheim Museum **has become** one of the most famous buildings in the world.* (= The change happened before now.)

*There **have been** some voices of opposition.*

Compare these present perfect and present simple forms:
*They **have invested** a lot of money in the area.* (= before now, we don't know if it's continuing)

*They **invest** a lot of money in the area.* (= generally)

*I've **had** a car for six years.* (= from six years ago to now)

*I **have** a car.* (= a present fact, time unknown)

Past perfect simple

The past perfect simple emphasises that something happened or started before another event or time in the past.

*The slum **had** effectively **created** a barrier between the affluent north and the more deprived south of the city.* (= before it was demolished)

*Up until the early 80s, Bilbao **had been dominated** by steel plants and shipbuilding.* (= before the 1980s)

Compare these past perfect and past simple forms:
*He had **gone** when I arrived.* (= He left before I arrived.)

*He **went** when I arrived.* (= First I arrived and at that moment he left.)

*He said **he'd been** a teacher.* (= When we spoke, he no longer taught.)

*He said he **was** a teacher.* (= When we spoke, he still taught.)

We also use the past perfect simple to refer to hypothetical events in the past (i.e. before now).

*If other mayors **hadn't secured** the city's finances before him, ...* (= The finances were secure.)

*I wish I **hadn't done** it, but I did.*

will have done (future perfect) and other modals

After a modal verb, we use infinitives without *to*. The perfect form is *will / may / should* + *have* + past participle.

*If we ever achieve a successful city for children, we **will have built** the perfect city for all citizens.* (= Before achieving it, you have to build it!)

*Other cities **may have failed** because they didn't take up the other strands of Bilbao's regeneration project.* (= before now; *may* shows possibility here)

*I **should have finished** work by six, but I'll call you if I haven't.*

Participle clauses

Sometimes we need an *-ing* form to form a participle clause.

***Having cleared** one space, Peñalosa's administration then expropriated the land of a private country club.* (= After they cleared / had cleared ...)

Compare these sentences:
*I was disappointed when I got there, **having read** so many good things about it.*

***Reading** about it now makes me want to go there.*

Exercise 1

Complete the pairs of sentences with the verbs in bold – one sentence with a perfect form, one not.

1 **not / call**
   a If I _____ by six, it means I'm not coming.
   b As a rule, I _____ anyone after nine at night.
2 **be done up**
   a It _____ a few years ago, but the place is already falling apart.
   b It used to be very run-down, but it _____.
3 **be struck**
   a It was the second time the city _____ by an earthquake.
   b Our house _____ by lightning last year.
4 **change**
   a I doubt anything _____ by this time next year.
   b I think things _____ if the Freedom Party wins power in the election.
5 **consult**
   a They should _____ the people who live here to find out what they want.
   b They should _____ more widely, but they just weren't interested in what others wanted and that's why the regeneration failed.
6 **be**
   a I wish he _____ here now.
   b It sounds like you had a great time. I wish I _____ there.
7 **spend**
   a _____ millions on the project, the city centre still looks awful!
   b _____ any amount of time there, you quickly start to feel stressed.
8 **undergo**
   a Following the disaster, the city _____ a huge transformation.
   b When the disaster struck, the city _____ a number of changes already.

Infinitive form

Sometimes we use an infinitive with *to* after certain verbs. Compare the perfect and simple forms:

*I **seem to have lost** my wallet.* (= before now)

*He **seems to lose** things all the time.* (= generally)

*He **is believed to have killed** several people.*

*He **is believed to be** dangerous.*

Exercise 2

Complete the second sentence so that it has a similar meaning to the first sentence using the word given. Do not change the word given. You must use between three and five words, including the word given.

1 I don't think my flight will get in in time to catch the last train home.
   LEFT
   The last train _____ the time my flight gets in.
2 The first time I saw anything like that was when I went to Mumbai.
   NEVER
   I _____ like that before I went to Mumbai.
3 I'm not sure I can give you any advice as it's so long since I've been there.
   RECENTLY
   Not _____, I don't think I can give you any advice.

4 When the current government came to power, they largely continued the previous government's policies.
   INITIATED
   The current government's policies _____ by the previous one.

5 People were moved out of the area before the storm hit so there were very few casualties.
   EVACUATED
   There would have been a lot more casualties if _____ before the storm.

6 As far as I can tell, things are much better than they were when I was there last.
   IMPROVED
   Things appear _____ since my last visit.

DID YOU KNOW?

We sometimes use *will / will have* to refer to the present to talk about what we believe.

*Many people **will have visited** the city just to see it and found a flourishing city with a vibrant nightlife. However, fewer **will be aware** of the profound change that the gallery symbolises.*

A: *Where are you from?*
B: *You **won't know** it. / You **won't have heard** of it. It's tiny.*

2 RELATIONSHIPS

WOULD

Conditionals

Would introduces the hypothetical result or consequence in a conditional sentence.

*I probably **would**'ve stayed with him if he'd apologised.*
*If they'd intervened, the situation **would** be a lot worse now.*
*If it hadn't been for my friend Andrew, I **would** never have got together with Ana.*

Would have + past participle refers back to a hypothetical past situation. Note that compared to *might*, *would* shows more certainty here.

Habits

We can use *would* instead of *used to* or the past simple to talk about habits in the past.

*When he was a toddler, I'**d** do the childcare most days.*
*Before the anger management classes, he'**d** often get into unnecessary confrontations.*

Note we also use *would* with *wish* to talk about present habits we (don't) want people to have.

*I wish he'**d** show a bit more commitment.*
*I wish they **wouldn't** interfere.*

Past of *will*

We use *would* as the past form of *will*. It tends to follow verbs such as *knew, said, thought, promised, threatened*, etc.

*I knew it **would** come to no good, but you can't really interfere, can you?*
*They said it **would** be miserable today, but it's actually turned out quite nice.*
*She promised she'**d** come, so I'm sure she'll be here soon.*

We often use *won't* to refuse to do something and so we use *would* to report it. Notice that this can also be applied to animals and machines!

*I remember once I asked him to change desks and he just **wouldn't** – just refused point blank.*
*For some reason, the car **wouldn't** start this morning so I'm waiting for the breakdown people.*

Advice

We use *I'd* to give advice. It sometimes goes with expressions such as *if I were you, if I were in your shoes*, etc., but it is more often used on its own.

*He should obviously be punished, but after that I'**d** still give him another chance.*
*I'**d** consider talking it over with a therapist.*

We sometimes use *would* in other advice expressions.

*I'**d** advise you to see a therapist.*
*I'**d** recommend taking a class.*
*You'**d** be best talking it over with someone.*

Being more cautious with opinions

We often use *I would / I wouldn't say* to introduce our opinions about people or a situation. Note we can also sometimes use *I would've said / I wouldn't have said* in the same way. These structures show more caution.

*I **would say** he has a stubborn streak and he's been prone to outbursts and answering back.*
*I **wouldn't say** it's a disaster – just a slight setback.*
*I **wouldn't have said** it's a big problem.*

Sometimes we use *would* to make a prediction or speculation sound more cautious. Compare the examples to the less cautious versions in brackets:

*Although he's a little frail now, I'**d expect** him to recover well.* (I expect him to …)
*I **don't imagine** there'**d be** a problem with that.* (I don't think there'll be a problem …)
*I'**d hope** to be back by six.* (I hope to be back by six.)
*I **would think** / I **would've thought** they'**d get married** at some point.* (I think they will get married …)

We also sometimes do this with requests because it can sound more polite.

***Would** it be OK to leave early?* (Is it OK to leave early?)
***Would** you **mind** helping me with this?* (Do you mind helping me with this?)

Exercise 1

Use *would*, the word in bold and up to four other words to complete the second sentence so it has the same meaning as the first sentence.

1 I'm completely with you on that.
   AGREE
   I _____ about that.

2 If you ask me, it wasn't his fault.
   SAY
   I _____ to blame.

3 We made several offers, but they rejected all of them.
   NOT
   They _____ our offers.

4 I think the best thing to do is walk away.
   INVOLVED
   I _____ if I were you.

5 He's always saying nasty things behind people's backs.
   BITCH
   I wish _____ behind their backs.

6 They shouldn't let him stay if he's going to behave like that.
   KICK
   If he behaved like that in my house, _____.

7 I'm unlikely to replace it.
   IMAGINE
   I _____ a new one.

8 It shouldn't take more than a week to arrive.
   EXPECT
   _____ get here before next Friday.

COMMON MISTAKES

We use *would* to talk about habits, but not about states like living, being, belonging, etc.

Before I moved to Birmingham, we ~~would live~~ **lived** in Leeds.

I sometimes wish I ~~would be~~ **was** taller.

When talking about habits or something we want to change in the future, we use *would* rather than past simple / *will*.

I wish he ~~stopped~~ **would** stop talking sometimes.

I wish it ~~will~~ **would** snow soon.

When reporting, we can use *will* if we think the action is still going to happen. Otherwise, we need to use *would*.

He promised he**'ll** give our assignments back tomorrow. ✓

He promised he ~~will~~ **would** be here on time today, but he was late again.

We don't use *would* or *would have* in the *if*-clause of a conditional sentence to refer to unreal events or situations. But we do use it if we are talking about a real past habit.

If I'd had a bad day at school, my gran **would** always comfort me. ✓ (= real past habit)

If he ~~would've~~ **had confided in** me, this wouldn't have happened.

Exercise 2

Decide which five sentences are incorrect, then correct them.

1 I didn't think I would enjoy the course, but the teacher has been great.
2 I often got into trouble at school just because I would have really long hair.
3 I'd hope that it'd be all sorted out pretty quickly.
4 My parents wish we would live a bit closer to them.
5 I wouldn't be here if I wouldn't have had the surgery.
6 I wouldn't have said it was a big problem.
7 Seriously, I wish my brother shut up sometimes.
8 I tried to talk him out of it, but he wouldn't listen and carried on.
9 It doesn't surprise me. I knew he'll say that! He's so predictable!
10 I would've thought it'd be fine if you arrive a little bit late.

3 CULTURE AND IDENTITY

CLEFT SENTENCES

We can change the structure of the standard subject–verb–object sentence in order to add emphasis. We often do this when correcting what we or someone else has just said.

Fronting

We can place the highlighted part at the front of the sentence starting with *It* and then add a relative clause.

He seems to be struggling with **the people**.
→ **It's the people** that he seems to be struggling with.

I didn't see him on **Monday**. I saw him on Tuesday.
→ **It wasn't Monday** I saw him; it was Tuesday.

I blame **the government** for the mess we're in.
→ **It's the government** who I blame for the mess we're in.

the thing, what, all, etc.

We often emphasise aspects of the sentence starting with *the thing, what,* etc. and then add a relative clause. The table below shows some of the most common ways to start the first clause. Notice the patterns in the second half of the sentence after *be*.

	First clause	*be*	Noun or noun phrase / clause
Emphasising how we feel	**The thing that** annoys me **One thing (that)** I find worrying **The main thing** I like **What** was great	is was	(the fact) that they did nothing. their stupidity. being able to do what I want. people's outlook on life. how quickly they solved the problem.
Emphasising an action with *do*	**All** we do **The only thing** he does **All** I did **What** they did in the end	is was	(to) sit around all day. (to) criticise. (to) question if he was right. (to) pretend it hadn't happened.
Emphasising an action with *happen*	**All that** happens **The only thing that** happened **What happened** in the end	is was	(that) people shout a bit. (that) I felt a bit awkward. (that) they fined me.
Emphasising a reason	**The reason why** they lost **The main reason** it happened	is was	(that) they didn't train enough. (that) no-one thought it could happen.
Emphasising a place	**The only place that's** worth visiting **The place (where)** you're most likely to find it	is	the castle. Harrods.

Exercise 1

Complete the exchanges with one word in each space.

1 A: I bet it's difficult to work in the summer there. It must be so hot.
   B: It is, although _____'s not really the heat _____'s the problem for me; it's the humidity.
2 A: What I liked about them _____ their humour and the _____ they took the mickey out of each other.
   B: Really? It's exactly that _____ I found difficult to relate to. It's just not my kind of thing.
3 A: Apparently, they don't want to work with me. All I _____ was _____ some ideas to make things more efficient.
   B: I know, but _____ you have to realise _____ that losing face is a big thing in their culture.
4 A: The _____ that bothers _____ about life these days is _____ everything revolves around money and consumption.
   B: Yeah, it depresses me too.
5 A: Sorry we're late. The traffic was bad.
   B: Don't listen to him. The real _____ we're late is that _____ spent an hour getting ready.
   A: It wasn't like that! What _____ was I _____ almost ready and then I spilt some tea on my trousers and I had to get changed.

Emphasising how we feel

When we emphasise how something makes us feel, we often use a 'feelings' verb rather than an adjective:

frustrates me	upsets me	I love
disturbs me	amazes me	I can't stand
scares me	drives me mad	I find difficult
bothers me	I find weird	

We also use a number of different noun phrases to start the second clause:

the way ...
the fact that ...
the number of ...
the amount of ...

What scares me most about it **is the amount of time** I know it's going to end up taking.

What I love most about her **is the way** she's so enthusiastic about everything all the time.

What I'm finding weirdest about my new job **is the fact that** I'm actually enjoying it!

Exercise 2

Complete the sentences with these pairs of words and phrases.

frustrates + lack	concerns + number
disturbs + stance	upset + seeing
amazes + amount	angered + the fact
drives + way	worrying + level

1 The main thing that _____ most people is the total _____ of investment in basic health care and education.

2 What _____ me the most while I was there was _____ all the kids sleeping on the streets.

3 One thing that _____ me is the government's _____ on law and order – and their emphasis on punishment.

4 One thing that really _____ me crazy is the _____ people queue up – or rather don't queue up!

5 What _____ me is the _____ of kids leaving school unable to read and write properly.

6 The thing I find most _____ is the _____ of pollution in the city. There's just a constant cloud of smog.

7 It's done now, I know, but what _____ me most was _____ that he didn't think he should even apologise!

8 What _____ me is the sheer _____ of wealth those at the top of society possess.

Exercise 3

Rewrite the sentences so they emphasise how you feel.

1 The city is very cosmopolitan, which surprised me.
One thing that _____.

2 He can be very nationalistic! It's very disturbing.
What _____.

3 The growing wealth gap is a concern.
The main thing that _____.

4 The whole society is ageing at an alarming rate. That's the really scary thing.
What _____.

5 People assume that I must love football just because I'm Brazilian. I get really angry about it.
One thing that _____.

---

4 POLITICS

CONDITIONALS 1

General truths

We can use conditionals to talk about things that are generally or always true. Both the *if*-clause and the result clause can use present tenses or *going to* + verb. The result clause can also use *will / should / might* and a number of other structures.

*If they**'re earning** that much, it **encourages** other people to ask for more.*

*If you **keep lying** to people, they**'re going to stop trusting** you after a while.*

*If you**'re going to be** late, you **should phone** me.*

*If you **don't like** them, **don't vote** for them.*

*If you really **want to understand** the situation there, you **need to read** more.*

Likely future events

We can also use conditionals to talk about likely / possible events in the future. The *if*-clause uses present tenses. The result clause often uses *going to* + verb / *will* + verb, but a number of other structures are also possible.

*Even if they **do manage** to introduce this new law, it**'s** basically **going to be** unworkable.*

*As long as there**'s** the official desire to make it work, then it**'ll work**.*

*If we**'re** lucky, we **can host** it without going into debt.*

*If they **make** further cuts, it**'s bound to lead to** job losses.*

*If they **win** the election, I **might have to leave** the country.*

*If you **have** the time, I**'d write** to your MP about it.*

Often the only way to work out whether a sentence is describing a general truth or a likely future event is by paying attention to vocabulary and context.

Imagined events now or in the future

We can use conditionals to talk about imagined / hypothetical events now or in the future. The *if*-clause uses past tenses. The result clause often uses *would / wouldn't* + verb, but *might / could* + verb are also possible.

*And what **would** you **include** in pay? Supposing they **were given** a boat, or whatever, instead of money?*

*Imagine if we actually **won** it. It**'d be** a recipe for disaster.*

*If they **raised** taxes, there**'d be** a riot.*

*I**'d quit** my job tomorrow if I **could**.*

*If she **weren't** so busy, she **could do** more for local people.*

Alternatives to *if*

As well as *if* there are other words used to introduce conditions.

Supposing (= what if / imagine if) *they were given a boat, or whatever, instead of money?*

Even if (= this condition does not change the result in any way) *they do manage to introduce this new law, it's basically going to be unworkable.*

Unless they (= if they don't) *come up with some new policy ideas, they're going to lose the election.*

*They'd better come up with some new policies **or** (= because if they don't) they'll lose the election.*

*They'd better come up with some new policies. **Otherwise**, (= if they don't) they're going to lose the election.*

*It's going to happen whether you want it to **or not!** (= It doesn't make any difference even if you want it to.)*

*What changes do you think the deal will lead to, **assuming** (= if it's true – and I think it is) that it goes ahead?*

As long as (= on condition that) *there's the official desire to make it work, then it'll work.*

So long as, provided and providing can all be used instead of as long as. They all mean the same thing.

Exercise 1

Complete the sentences with one word in each space. Contractions count as one word.

1 If it all goes wrong, _____ say I didn't warn you.

2 Supposing they do more to stop petty crime, it's _____ to have a knock-on effect on more serious crimes.

3 If you go there at night, I _____ take someone with you. It's a rough area.

4 If the softer approach is failing, maybe they _____ adopt a tougher position.

5 People here would _____ put up with a law like that. There _____ be riots!

6 People complain about public services, but then they moan if the government _____ up taxes.

7 If they _____ what they were doing, I'd have more faith, but they obviously _____.

8 You're very calm! I'd _____ furious if I _____ in your situation.

9 A: I see they're promising to cut taxes.
   B: I hope they do! To be honest, I don't think I _____ vote for them if they _____.

10 A: The papers are full of stories about his personal life.
   B: Maybe it's just me, but I honestly _____ care whether he _____ done any of those things or not.

11 A: I read somewhere that the prime minister is thinking of signing a new gas deal with them.
   B: I know. It's a terrible idea. If he _____, there _____ be huge protests against it.

12 A: I know it's never going to happen, but if you ask me, they should just ban junk food.
   B: Oh, come on! That's a bit extreme. Imagine what _____ happen if they _____!

Exercise 2

Complete the second sentence so that it has a similar meaning to the first sentence using the word given. Do not change the word given. You must use between three and five words, including the word given.

1 They won't achieve anything without popular support.
   UNLESS
   _____, they won't achieve anything.

2 I'm in favour of the idea so long as it's not too expensive.
   PROVIDED
   I basically support the idea, _____ too much money.

3 It doesn't matter if you don't like it. That doesn't stop it happening, does it!
   WHETHER
   It's always going to happen, _____ not!

4 The problem with nuclear power is that if an accident happens, it could totally devastate the area.
   SUPPOSING
   _____ at a nuclear power plant. Can you imagine the damage it could cause?

5 The economy's still doing badly so it's easy for the opposition to attract new supporters.
   LONG
   The opposition will continue to win new supporters _____ fails to improve.

6 There's no way the situation will improve without immediate action being taken.
   OR
   They need to do something pretty soon _____ worse and worse.

7 I know opinion polls aren't entirely reliable, but it doesn't look like they'll win an overall majority.
   ASSUMING
   _____ reliable, they're going to have to form a coalition with someone.

CONDITIONALS 2

General past truths

To talk about things that were generally true in the past, both the *if*-clause and the result clause can use past tenses. The result clause also often uses *would* + verb.

*It **helped** the programme's ratings if they **had** a kind of hate figure. (= They had a hate figure and this boosted the show's popularity.)*

*If there **was** a school council election, all these posters **would go up** all over the place. (= Every time there was an election, this is what always happened.)*

Imagined events in the past

To talk about imagined events in the past, the *if*-clause uses past perfect tenses. To talk about imagined past results, the result clause often uses *would / wouldn't + have + past participle.*

*If they'**d called** on another day, I **wouldn't have taken part**. (= In reality, they called on a day I wasn't busy and so I took part.)*

*I **might never have heard of** him if he **hadn't been taking part** in that radio show. (= He was taking part in a radio show and that's when I first encountered him.)*

Imagined events in both the past and the present

If the *if*-clause uses the past perfect, it is about an imagined past. If the *if*-clause uses the past simple / continuous, it is about an imagined present.

If the result clause uses *would / might / could + have + past participle* (or *would / might / could + have been + -ing*), it's about an imagined past result.

If the result clause uses *would / might / could + verb* (or *would / might / could + be + -ing*), it's about an imagined present result.

*I **might not have minded** so much if the calls **were** free, but they're making a fortune on them. (= I minded / I was angry in the past because generally / still now the calls aren't free – they cost a lot!)*

*If they **hadn't been** so reluctant to negotiate, we **would not be taking** this action now. (= The reason we are taking action now is because in the past they were reluctant to negotiate.)*

*It's unlikely we **would've abolished** uniforms if we **didn't have** a body like this. (= It's because generally / still now we have a student council that we were able to abolish uniforms in the past.)*

Exercise 1

Complete the sentences with the correct form of the verbs. In some cases, it may be possible to use more than one modal verb. Use the modal verb that makes most sense in the context.

1 They _____ (win) the election by a landslide if they _____ (change) their leader. As it was though, they won a very narrow victory.

2 In the end, I voted for the Liberals in the last election. I _____ (vote) Social Democrats, but I _____ (not / like) their stance on nuclear power. It just seemed very old-fashioned, to be honest.

3 He _____ (be) president now if he _____ (not / be mixed up) in that big scandal last year.

4 We _____ (not / be) as developed as we are today if she _____ (not / make) such radical changes when she was in power.

5 If the last government _____ (not / give) the banks so much power, we _____ (not / be) in this mess today! Honestly, I hold them responsible for all of it.

6 She really helped me a lot when I was at high school. If I _____ (need) someone to talk to, she _____ (be) there for me. If I _____ (have) problems, I _____ (go) and see her. She was amazing.

Exercise 2

Decide which options below are possible.

1 If I'd been told, ...
   a there wouldn't have been a problem.
   b we wouldn't be in this mess, would we?
   c I decided earlier.
   d I'd be doing something about it.
   e I had reported it to the police.

2 If we hadn't reported it when we did, ...
   a someone could've been seriously hurt.
   b we weren't sleeping afterwards.
   c the police hadn't known about it.
   d it'd be a health hazard.
   e we wouldn't have been able to forgive ourselves if and when something happened.

3 If we had a better system in place, ...
   a we wouldn't need to be having this inquiry.
   b none of this happened.
   c more incidents like this one could be stopped.
   d this had been stopped before it got so serious.
   e this might never have happened.

4 If there was an accident at the power plant, ...
   a I dread to think of the consequences.
   b there was going to be an official investigation into the causes.
   c I'd rather not be around!
   d you can expect a lot of casualties.
   e it'd show they hadn't been taking proper security measures.

5 GOING OUT, STAYING IN

NOUN PHRASES

We can add to basic nouns in the following ways.

Adding information before nouns

Names and the kinds of things they are

We often add the name of something to the kind of thing it is (or vice versa). No linker or relative clause is needed.

Visit the 18th-century stately home, Kenwood House, ...

We've chosen The Hackney Empire, a theatre ...

Compound nouns

Nouns can act like adjectives and define other nouns. The first noun isn't made plural.

cream teas   the boat race

Adjectives

Adjectives usually go before nouns (but see reduced relative clauses below). We don't tend to use more than three adjectives before a noun. As a general rule, we give opinions first, then facts.

classic English cream teas

cool young things

our best multicultural cheap eats

We sometimes make compound adjectives with number + noun. The noun is not plural.

a five-mile walk

a six-hour course

We also sometimes make compound adjectives instead of relative clauses (see below).

*... best known for it's **award-winning** Christmas pantomimes.*
(= pantomimes that have won awards)

Adding information after nouns

Prepositional phrases

You can add phrases beginning with a preposition after nouns. We can use them to show:

• where something is.

*a five-mile walk **up a steep hill***

• what it has or contains.

*Hampstead Heath **with its natural ponds***

*an 18th-century stately home **with a fine collection of art***

Some nouns collocate strongly with particular prepositions.

*increasing **interest in** politics*

Relative clauses

We can add a clause to the noun to explain what it is or to add extra information.

*the Geffrye Museum, **which contains living rooms from different periods***

*a theatre **that once hosted Charlie Chaplin***

Reduced relative clauses

We often shorten relative clauses with present (-ing) participles or past participles. The present participle replaces active forms. The past participle replaces passives.

*four period gardens **which show** changing trends* →	*four period gardens **showing** changing trends*
*a classic 'chippie' **which is run** by second-generation Greek immigrants* →	*a classic 'chippie' **run** by second-generation Greek immigrants*
*its great Zoo Late evenings, **which are held** throughout the summer* →	*its great Zoo Late evenings, **held** throughout the summer*

Sometimes we reduce the relative clause to an adjectival phrase.

*one of the hippest places in town, **which is full** of trendy bars* →	*one of the hippest places in town, **full** of trendy bars*

Exercise 1

Underline the most basic subject, verb and object in the sentences.

1 The Oscar-winning director Joel Riley, whose latest documentary *Sick Life* is currently on release, gives a talk at the Barbican tonight, explaining his take on the current state of the film industry in the UK.

2 From its fourth-century origins in the deserts of the Middle East, through the many and varied forms of religious life it assumed during the Middle Ages, the tradition of a life of solitary retreat is explored in depth in this latest book by award-winning writer Denise Lawrenson.

3 The parents of two troubled teenagers who were caught at the scene of a robbery in Georgetown, supposedly after listening to subliminal messages in the music of their favourite band Death House, are seeking an as-yet-unspecified amount of damages in compensation from the thrash metal group concerned and their record label.

Exercise 2

Add the phrases in the box to the two nouns in the basic sentence below.

John Moffit stars in *The Dying*.

character actor	the three-hour
road movie	37-year-old
from Canada	award-winning
action-packed	by Tom Daley
based on the book	playing in his first lead role

Exercise 3

Shorten all the relative clauses as much as possible. You may need to use a present participle.

1 Visit the awe-inspiring cathedral which was designed by the architect Antonio Gaudi.

2 I read a fascinating article in the paper by the novelist whose name is Anne Tyler.

3 The exhibitions which are held in the centre are accompanied by workshops which are suitable for all ages.

4 There are a wealth of exhibits which are on show, which date back thousand of years.

Exercise 4

Rewrite the sentences using noun phrases in each space.

1 The course lasts six weeks and teaches a number of guidelines. If you follow them, you will be able to lose weight quickly and effectively.
_____ provides guidelines for _____.

2 When arms are supplied to other countries, the matter often causes controversy.
The _____ is a _____.

3 They want to create a new car tax, but a lot of people are opposed to the idea.
There's _____ to the _____.

4 The monument was built to celebrate the fact Jonson had been born a hundred years earlier.
The _____ celebrated the _____ anniversary _____.

6 CONFLICT AND RESOLUTION

WISH AND IF ONLY

We use *wish* and *if only* to talk about hypothetical situations – things we want but which are impossible. They are followed by *would*, the past perfect, the past simple or *could*. Often only the auxiliaries of these tenses and structures are used with *wish* / *if only*. *I wish* is more commonly used than *if only*.

if only / *wish* + would(n't)

This explains how you want people to behave differently.
If only you**'d** put things away properly!
*I **wish** you **wouldn't** shout.*
A: *It's a shame he doesn't cook more often.*
B: *I know – I **wish** he **would**. He's really good.*

if only / *wish* + past perfect

This explains how you would like the past to be different. Use *could've* + past participle to refer to an ability to do something. We often just use the auxiliary *had*.
*I **wish** you**'d said** something sooner.*
B: *I was going to take it to my room.*
A: *Well, I **wish** you **had** (taken it to your room).*
A: *I **wish** I **could've done** more to help.*
B: *You did more than enough. Thanks.*

if only / *wish* + past simple / could

This refers to things in the present that we want to be different. We may use the auxiliaries *was / were*, *did* or *could*.
A: *Can you give me a hand later?*
B: *I **wish** I **could**, but I'm working tonight.*
A: *Sorry, I have to go.*
B: ***If only*** you **didn't**! I was planning on making us dinner.*
D: *What? You're joking?*
C: *I **wish** I **was** / **were**.*

Note that in spoken English *I wish I was* is more common than *I wish I were*. However, some people think *I wish + were* is more correct. In more formal situations, it may be better to use *I wish I / you / he / she were*.

wish and replies

When replying to *wish* / *if only* comments, we may want to talk about real situations – or continue to refer to the hypothetical situation. This affects the use of tenses.
C: *I **wish** you**'d said** something sooner.*
D: *I **would have** (said something, if I'd had the opportunity = a hypothetical situation), but you hardly come out of that office.*
A: ***If only*** we **had** more money!*
B: *Yeah, well we **don't** (have more money = a real situation), so we **need** to find some other solution.*
A: *I **wish** you**'d tell** me if there's a problem.*
B: *I **would** (tell you = a hypothetical situation), but you**'ve been** so dismissive when I **have** (told you = a real situation) in the past!*

Exercise 1

Complete the exchanges with the correct auxiliary verbs. You may need a contraction such as *didn't* or *would've*.

1 A: I thought you were going to ask him to help?
B: I wish I _____. I just got distracted with other things.
A: It's a shame you _____ – we _____ been able to sort this out a lot quicker.

2 A: Are you going away during the holidays?
B: If only I _____, but I don't really have the money.
A: I wish I _____ lend you some, but I'm in the same boat.
B: Maybe we _____ win the lottery!

3 A: I seriously wish I _____ never even mentioned the issue. It's not really a problem.
B: Oh, don't worry. He _____ found something else to complain about anyway.
A: That's true. If only he _____ such a control freak.
B: I know. Work _____ be a lot easier.

4 A: You know I'm leaving tomorrow, don't you?
B: Yeah. I wish you _____. I _____ miss you.
A: Well, I wish I _____ stayed longer, but I have to get back.

5 A: I really wish you _____ invited him.
B: I _____ have, but the other day you said you felt sorry for him.
A: I do – kind of – I just wish he _____ stand there staring at people. It's a bit creepy.

Exercise 2

Complete the second sentence so that it has a similar meaning to the first sentence using the word given. Do not change the word given. You must use between three and six words, including the word given.

1 I really regret speaking to her like that.
ONLY
If _____ to her like that!

2 Not being able to go to university has been one of my big regrets in life.
COULD
I really _____ to university, but it just wasn't possible.

3 It annoys me that you get so upset over such a small thing.
WISH
I _____ over-sensitive about everything.

4 Basically, I'd like everyone to get along better.
FIGHT
I wish people _____ much.

5 It's a shame we have to work today.
NOT
I wish _____ work today.

6 It's no good you telling me that now!
IF
_____ that earlier!

7 SCIENCE AND RESEARCH

PASSIVES

Passives focus attention on who or what an action affects. We often use them when the subject of the sentence is not the doer or cause of the action. This is because the doer is either unimportant, obvious or unknown.

Different tenses

We're surrounded by statistics. (present simple)
Company B's actually being hugely outperformed. (present continuous)
It was published anonymously on the Web. (past simple)
The figures were obviously being twisted. (past continuous)
The article has been published in several well-respected journals. (present perfect simple)
Researchers had been pressured to come up with positive results. (past perfect simple)

Note that passive constructions aren't usually used in the present perfect continuous or the past perfect continuous.

Passives after modal verbs

We can form passives after modal verbs using *be* + past participle.
Statistics can be used to manipulate.
The data will be thoroughly analysed by a team of experts.
Similar results should have been seen, but for some reason weren't.
The research must have been funded by someone with a vested interest in the results.

get passives

With some verbs, *get* is often used instead of *be*. This is more common in informal spoken language than in academic writing or journalism. *Get* passives often show an action was unexpected or accidental.
Researchers may get pressured into finding positive results.
Thousands get hurt every year in avoidable accidents.
The laboratory got broken into and vandalised.

have something done

We often use a form of the verb *have* + past participle to talk about services we arrange and pay for.
A food company is having some research done.
The fish have cancerous cells inserted in their bodies.
My uncle had a kidney removed.

Note that we can also use *get* in this way. *Get* is more common with some verbs, *have* with others. There are no rules for this. It's best to just learn from examples you meet.
I got my legs waxed the other day.
I got my jacket caught in the closing door.

Reporting

In academic writing and journalism, we often use reporting verbs in the passive form where the source is unimportant or to suggest a degree of uncertainty.
So next, statistics – often thought to be the worst kind of lying there is!
The disease is believed to have a genetic component.
The government is said to be considering an enquiry.
It is argued that the research could provide a breakthrough.
He is alleged to have faked the experiments.

-ing forms

We use *-ing* passive forms after prepositions and some verbs.
They may worry about not being employed again.
It was accepted for publication after being reviewed by other experts.
I hate being interviewed.

Reduced relative clauses

If passives are used in relative clauses, the relative pronoun and the verb *be* are often left out.
Obviously, research in a respected journal, ~~which has been~~ reviewed by other experts, will be better than something ~~that is / has been~~ published anonymously online.
A paper ~~that was~~ published recently seems to prove a causal link.
The sample group consisted of people ~~who had been~~ chosen at random.

Avoiding passives

In more informal spoken English, we often use *you* or *they* to avoid passives.
You can buy tickets online. (= Tickets can be bought online.)
They've demolished the building. (= The building has been demolished.)
You could use statistics to manipulate people if you wanted to. (= Statistics could be used to manipulate ...)

Exercise 1

Complete the second sentence with a passive construction so it has the same meaning as the first sentence.

1 They've achieved a breakthrough in nanotechnology.
A breakthrough in nanotechnology _____.
2 They gave me an injection before they stitched the cut up.
I _____ and then they stitched the cut up.
3 Scientists believe this technique is the way forward.
This technique _____ the way forward.
4 The dentist took one of my wisdom teeth out.
I _____ out.
5 It's vital that thorough research supports policy.
Policy should always _____ thorough research.
6 In the end, he got employment as a researcher with the FBI.
He ended up _____ the FBI as a researcher.
7 Some think a mineral deficiency causes the disorder.
The disorder _____ deficiency.
8 The government should fund our research.
Our research needs _____ the government.

DID YOU KNOW

Need + -ing is a passive construction and can be used instead of *need / have to be done*.
*The phenomenon **needs investigating** (OR **needs to be investigated**) further.*
*My house desperately **needs repainting** (OR **needs to be repainted**).*

Exercise 2

Complete the sentences with the correct form (active or passive) of the verbs.

1 The research, which is due to be completed sometime next year, _____ by Tokyo University. (carry out)
2 The government says that since the outbreak started, those _____ have received full treatment, while all those in vulnerable groups _____. (affect, vaccinate)
3 Scientists _____ the research are confident it will lead to clean renewable energy that can _____ at a competitive price. (undertake, produce)
4 The results can't _____ by anything other than the people in the area _____ to radiation in the area for a number of years. (cause, expose)
5 After _____ from the organ, the sample tissue _____ for the disease and the results came out negative. (extract, test)
6 While the failure of the initial probe _____ the exploration of Mars, it _____ that the lessons learnt will _____ other problems further down the line. (set back, hope, prevent)

8 NATURE AND NUTURE

AUXILIARIES

Auxiliaries are words like *be, have, do, will, must,* etc. that we use to make negatives and questions. We also use them to avoid repetition and to add emphasis.

Questions

We use auxiliaries to form normal questions such as *Do you like it?* and *Have you been there?* We also use auxiliaries to form tag questions at the end of statements as well as short responses and rhetorical questions.

*After all, women are better communicators, **aren't they**?*

*Baron-Cohen's choice is simply based on the fact jobs in such fields have traditionally been occupied by women. And why **have they**?*

Tags

We often use tags to ask genuine questions to check things or to make polite requests. However, we also use tags when giving an opinion we expect people to agree with. Positive sentences normally have negative tags and negative statements use a positive tag.

*It was great, **wasn't it**?*

*You've never been there, **have you**?*

*You couldn't lend me your phone for a minute, **could you**?*

DID YOU KNOW?

We sometimes use a positive statement with a positive tag to express surprise or anger.

*Oh, you've got a son, **have you**? Why didn't I know that?*

*You want to borrow some money, **do you**? You haven't paid me back from last time yet!*

Short questions

We often use short auxiliary questions as responses to show interest and continue the conversation.

A: *I spent a month in Mongolia.*

B: ***Did you**?*

A: *Yeah, it was great. I went there as part of my degree.*

A: *I don't really like travelling.*

B: ***Don't you**? How come?*

Avoiding repetition

Auxiliaries help us to avoid repeating a verb or verb phrase we've already used.

*When talking to a boss, we won't butt in, but they **will** ~~butt in~~.*

Research in the journal Science *has shown both sexes talk equally as much, and in ~~talking equally as much~~ **doing** so use on average 16,000 words per day.*

*How people communicate has far more to do with social status and power than it ~~has to do~~ **does** with genetic make-up and 'nature'.*

Note that we sometimes need a different form of the auxiliary to the verb phrase we are replacing.

A: ***I'm not coming** tomorrow.*

B: ***Aren't** you (coming)? I thought you **were** (coming).*

A: *Yeah, I thought I **might** (come), but I've got to work.*

A: ***Did** you **speak** to him?*

B: *No, but I wish I **had** (spoken to him). It would've saved a lot of time.*

so and nor

When we avoid repetition with an auxiliary after *so / nor / neither*, the subject and auxiliary are reversed.

***We don't recycle** very much, but then **neither does anyone else** round here, apparently.*

A: ***We have foxes** living in our garden.*

B: *Really? **So do I**!*

Emphasising

Auxiliaries can add emphasis. We often add emphasis when we are contradicting what someone has said or written. In speech, we do this by stressing the auxiliary. If there's no auxiliary, we add *do / does / did*.

*Finally, if these supposed language differences **were** biological, we would expect ...*

*Some men **do** speak over others more, but this is not to do with gender.*

We also use auxiliaries in emphatic tags (see page 71).

*I'd love to go there, I really **would**.*

Exercise 1

Complete the exchanges with the correct auxiliaries. You will need to use negatives.

1 A: I'm not keen on zoos.
   B: Neither _____ I, but my kids _____, which is why we're going.

2 A: I'm a bit scared your dog will bite me.
   B: Don't worry. He _____. He's always pretty friendly.

3 A: That fish really _____ look very strange indeed!
   B: It _____, _____ it?!

4 A: He's always butting in!
   B: I know. I really wish he _____.

5 A: The car will be OK on the dirt roads, _____ it?
   B: Yeah, I would think so.

6 A: I hated the place, I really _____! I wouldn't go back there again.
   B: _____ you? What was so terrible about it?

7 A: My car's at the garage at the moment. If it _____, I'd come and get you from the airport, but I _____, I'm afraid.
   B: Don't worry about it. What's the problem with it, anyway?

8 A: Have you fed the dog?
   B: No I _____, but I _____ in a minute, OK?

9 A: Didn't you say at one point that you were going to Poland this summer?
   B: I _____, yeah – and I still _____. I just haven't sorted out all the details yet.

Exercise 2

Add an auxiliary verb in the correct place in each sentence (and make any other changes necessary) to emphasise the opinions.

1 He lives up to that stereotype of a macho man who hardly speaks.

2 Don't get me wrong. I liked the country to visit. It's just too dry and barren to really live there.

3 My son really enjoys playing with dolls, but I think that's fine.

4 The female of the species participates in the raising of the young, but it's predominantly a male job.

5 Tigers used to be quite common in the area, but they've been hunted to the verge of extinction.

6 He talks over you a bit, but his wife is worse!

Exercise 3

Write responses that contradict the statements.

1 A: You never told me you'd been to Venezuela.
   B: _____. You must have forgotten.

2 A: It looks a bit like a chicken.
   B: _____. It looks more like a swan, or something.

3 A: There's no way we'll get there on time.
   B: _____ – if you just start driving a bit faster!

4 A: It never really gets that cold there.
   B: _____. It actually snowed the year before last.

5 A: I don't think it's an endangered species.
   B: _____. I read there were only 400 left in the wild.

INFORMATION FILES

Group A

BOGOTA

The ex-mayor of Bogota, Enrique Peñalosa, has argued that if we ever achieve a successful city for children, we will have built the perfect city for all citizens. In Bogota, the capital of Colombia, they have tried to fulfil this ideal by transforming what was once a chaotic city – badly affected by congestion and gripped by fear of crime – into one far better for children. Peñalosa is largely credited with this transformation through the **large-scale reforms** he initiated at the turn of the century. However, if other mayors hadn't secured the city's finances before him and developed his reforms afterwards, the changes wouldn't have been so successful.

One of the first steps he took was to **clear a large slum** that dominated the centre of Bogota and replace it with a large public space. The slum had been a no-go zone for police and had effectively **created a barrier** between the affluent north and the more deprived south of the city. By demolishing it, the city was immediately brought closer together. Having cleared one space, Peñalosa's administration then **expropriated the land** of a private country club in the north of the city. Its golf course and polo fields were converted into a free park with sports facilities for all.

They then started to **tackle congestion** and the lack of facilities for pedestrians and cyclists. Wide pavements were built and cars were prevented from parking on them – a move that led to huge **protests**. The government built miles and miles of cycle lanes and set up a huge network of buses, again using separate lanes. They also **imposed restrictions** on car use and increased taxes on petrol, the proceeds from which went back into the new transport system.

Finally, they **poured money into** education – building new schools and a network of libraries, several in the most deprived neighbourhoods. The schools were also given thousands of computers connected to both the Internet and the libraries. The programme resulted in a huge **increase in enrolment** and school attendance.

During his time in office, Peñalosa did not **escape criticism** and after his three-year term in office, he failed to be re-elected in subsequent attempts. Some critics hate aspects of the road laws; others complain new housing is far from their original home in the city centre.

Student B

A friend of a friend of mine heard this story from a guy he met in Ireland.

Apparently, there was a student who was trying to get home from a party one night. He'd missed the last bus and so decided to hitchhike. It was pouring with rain and he'd been waiting for ages so when he saw a car coming slowly towards him, he just jumped in.

He soon realised, though, that there was nobody behind the wheel and the engine wasn't running. The car carried on moving slowly and as they neared a curve in the road, a hand appeared through the window and turned the wheel. By this point, the student was terrified so when he saw the lights of a café come into view, he leapt out and ran to safety. He rushed inside and started telling everybody about the horrible experience he had just had.

Then the door opened again and two more men walked in from the dark and stormy night. Looking around and seeing the shaking student, one said to the other, 'Look, James ... there's that idiot that got in the car while we were pushing it!'

Student B

1   Your neighbours seem to be going through a very rough patch and are constantly shouting. You've just heard several things being smashed and a woman screaming 'Stop it! Stop it!' at the top of her voice.

2   You've had a few problems with a project at work through no fault of your own, but you think a colleague has been going behind your back in order to undermine you and get your job.

3   The doctor wants to discharge a member of your family from hospital, but you aren't convinced they are ready to come home and you're not sure if you'll cope.

Group B

MANCHESTER

On 15th June 1996, a huge bomb in Manchester, in the north-west of England, **devastated the city centre**, causing nearly a billion pounds' worth of damage. The bomb, which had been planted by a terrorist group called the IRA, injured over 200 people but remarkably killed no-one as police had **evacuated the area** following a warning from the IRA.

Manchester had already **undergone some changes** as it recovered from the recession of the early 1990s that had destroyed much of its industry and created large-scale unemployment. It had won the right to **host the Commonwealth Games** (a large sporting event) and redeveloped some deprived areas through the building of the National Velodrome, an exhibition centre and an award-winning concert hall. However, at the time of the bombing, the city centre was still **badly neglected** – dominated by the hideous Arndale Shopping Centre (once described as looking like an enormous public toilet) and squares that were run-down and affected by drug addiction. So, dreadful though the bombing was, it actually provided an opportunity to start again that might not have happened otherwise.

Within weeks of the explosion, the government had set up a public-private company to manage the recovery and **launched an international competition** to design the redevelopment. The winning plan involved restoring the historic buildings that had been damaged, demolishing and rebuilding some of the ugly buildings, creating new public spaces and improving life for pedestrians. Alongside this, the council reduced traffic in the centre by **diverting main roads** and developed an integrated public transport system, making access to the centre easier. Since these improvements, the city has attempted to **boost tourism** by using some of the city's historical sites for major public events and by creating the Urbis building, which now houses the National Museum of Football. In turn, these changes have been **key in attracting** new investors, such as the Qatari royal family who own Manchester City Football Club.

Since 1996, the Manchester economy has grown in all areas. However, there are some concerns that **inequality has also increased**. Nor are all the new spaces appreciated. One new garden square designed by an international architect was rated as the worst attraction in the city. Others argue that in swapping market stalls and industry for luxury consumption and sparkling glass buildings, the city has **lost some of its soul**.

Oldbury is a town of 250,000. It is to receive £500 million of funding to halt the decline that has been taking place over a number of years. There's a chemical works on the outskirts of the town which produces nasty fumes. The city has a number of deprived areas and high unemployment. The small historical centre, which is very run-down, dates back 300 years.

Ideas for improving Oldbury

- set up a recycling centre
- provide grants for people starting up new businesses
- restore the historical centre and build a tourist centre
- provide low-interest loans to improve homes
- shut down the chemical works and relocate it on the coast
- set up youth centres to give young unemployed people something to do and to keep them off the street
- recruit more officers to police the poorer parts of the city
- plant trees in every street and increase the amount of green space available for public use

Student C

1 You have been assigned to collaborate with a new classmate on an assessed project, but you find her quite hard work. She doesn't contribute much to discussions and you feel she's not pulling her weight in other ways.

2 Your best friend has started going out with someone who from the first moment got on your nerves. It's difficult to put your finger on why you just don't like him / her, but recently you've had the feeling that maybe he / she fancies you!

3 You think your husband / wife is too soft with your children and far too indulgent. You often refuse to buy the children things and you set clear rules, but then they go to your husband / wife and he / she gives in immediately and undermines you.

FILE 5

Unit 1 page 13   SPEAKING

Student A

A friend of one of my cousins told me this story.

Outside the zoo in his city there's this big car park. It must hold something like 150 cars and maybe ten or fifteen coaches. They charge cars £2 to park and coaches £5. Anyway, there was this really nice parking attendant working there who used to make jokes and smile and everyone loved him. This guy must have been there for something like 25 years all in all. And then one day he just didn't turn up for work. It was like he'd vanished.

The zoo called the local council to let them know and to request a new parking attendant, but you can imagine their surprise when they were told that the parking area was *their* responsibility. They queried this and said surely the council employed the attendant. 'No,' came the answer, 'we'd always assumed you did!'

Somewhere, in a far-off distant land, there must be a retired man who'd been taking around £400 a day, seven days a week, for the last two decades. He must have taken well over two million pounds!

And no-one even knows his name!

FILE 11

Unit 4 page 36   UNDERSTANDING VOCABULARY

Student A

A poor desperate man is *looking* into a bin desperately searching for something to sell to buy some food. Then a man *goes* past him on the street and *looks* at the poor man as if he's awful and worthless. The man is obviously wealthy – he's *holding* an expensive leather briefcase; he's *talking* on a top smartphone, and the poor man also spots he's wearing a Rolex watch. The poor man's absolutely desperate and angry at the way the wealthy man *looked* at him, so he *goes* up behind him, *holds* his neck and *says*, 'Give me all your money!' The wealthy man *says*, 'You can't do this to me, I'm a Member of Parliament.' To which the poor man replies, 'Well in that case, just give me back MY money!'

FILE 15

Unit 7 page 63   CONVERSATION PRACTICE

Student A

Article 1

Two male penguins are rearing a chick together after they were given an egg to look after. The male pair had previously been seen imitating heterosexual behaviour and zookeepers wanted to see how they would react to real fatherhood. The pair immediately sheltered the egg and saw it hatch. They have since continued to look after it and behave as a normal mother and father. Zoologists say that homosexual-type behaviour is quite common in animals of all kinds.

FILE 7

Unit 2 page 21   SPEAKING

Student A

1 Two good friends of yours have fallen out badly. You're having a few friends over for your birthday and would like them both to come, but you don't want a scene or bad atmosphere between them to spoil the evening.

2 Your father is looking after your mother, who is very frail and unsteady on her feet, but he himself has become very forgetful and is struggling to cope.

3 Your son takes a very laid-back attitude to his studies and although he's taken things in his stride so far, you're worried he might fall behind and fail.

FILE 13

Unit 6 page 53   CONVERSATION PRACTICE

Student A

Conversation 1
You share a house with Student B and three other people. For some time now, you've felt that Student B doesn't really fit in, but you don't want to find someone else at this point. He / She always complains about the noise and about everyone else's inability to stick to the rota of household chores, yet doesn't seem to realise his / her own failings. He / She has a short temper and frequently ends up screaming and shouting or slamming doors after rows. Start the conversation by saying 'Good morning' to Student B and asking, 'How are you?' Try to work through the issues with your partner and find a solution to the dispute.

Conversation 2
You work for an import-export company. You really like the company and want to stay but have had problems with Student B, who is your line manager. He / She has asked to have a word with you. You've felt for some time that Student B sometimes picks on you and a few months ago you reported what you felt had been bullying behaviour to the regional manager. You fear Student B is still angry about this. However, you're also worried it could be about a company event you attended recently where you ended up talking to a colleague and mentioned some new plans for the company. You now realise you shouldn't have talked about the plans. Your partner will start the conversation. Try to clear the air while making clear how you feel.

Article 2

A Californian company, My DNA Fragrance, is producing scents based on the DNA of famous dead people such as Marilyn Monroe, Elvis Presley, Einstein and Michael Jackson. The DNA has been extracted from pieces of hair that have been acquired by John Reznikoff, who has the world's largest collection of hair from famous people dating back to the sixteenth century. The company says that the resulting fragrance is the 'essence' of the star rather than being their actual smell but that the process is entirely scientific. The perfume varies in price but on average costs around $90.

FILE 12

Student B

A politician goes and visits one of his counterparts in another country and they're *going* round the garden of his colleague's house. The place is beautiful! The garden has a heated swimming pool, a tennis court and a lovely lawn; the house has three storeys, six bedrooms – it's fantastic! The visiting politician *says*, 'Wow, they must pay MPs a lot more here than in my country.' His host laughs and *says*, 'Not really ... but you look at that motorway over there.' The visiting politician *looks* into the distance and *spots* a brand-new six-lane motorway with a few cars speeding along it. He turns back to his colleague who simply *laughs*, winks and pats his pocket. And then the light bulb goes on in the head of the overseas guest, who *says*, 'Say no more!'

Anyway, a few months later, the politician's counterpart returns the visit and comes to see him at his home. He's amazed when he sees the house. He's speechless! He just *looks* at the four-storey mansion, the ten bedrooms, the lovely grounds around it with a huge swimming pool, a sauna, a Jacuzzi, two tennis courts. Then there's a Rolls Royce and a Ferrari parked outside. Eventually, he *says*, 'But ... but I thought you said that MPs were badly paid here.' And the politician *laughs* and says, 'Well, you know, have a look at that new motorway over there.' And his foreign counterpart *looks* into the distance and scans the horizon, 'But there's nothing there.' And the politician just *laughs*, winks and pats his pocket.

FILE 14

Student B

Conversation 1

You share a house with Student A and three other people. You like the house – it's in a great location and is good value. However, you have issues with some of your housemates. It's Tuesday morning and you haven't slept very well because someone was playing music and chatting loudly until 2am. You have exams next week and feel your housemates are being inconsiderate. You are also generally fed up with how messy everyone else is and are really reaching your limit! You've come down to the kitchen to make some coffee. Student A will start a conversation with you. Try to persuade them to establish some rules.

Conversation 2

You have recently been appointed departmental manager for an import-export company. You get on badly with Student A, who works under you in the company. You have reason to believe he / she has revealed information about a forthcoming deal because a friend in a different department heard it mentioned at a recent social event. You're worried it could be a much bigger problem if the plans become more widely known. You also feel he / she often undermines you and have not forgotten that a few months ago you had words. Student A went over your head and complained about you to the regional manager. Start the conversation by raising your worries. You want to establish a better working relationship.

FILE 10

UNDERSTANDING FAST SPEECH

Groups of words are marked with / and pauses are marked //. Stressed sounds are in CAPITALS.

Video 1 page 22

I need a LONG DIStance / to MAKE a TURN NOW / like I CAN'T / there's NO WAY I could MAKE ONE of these TURNS down these STREETS / I'm going to have to GO DOWN // and cut Over THREE LANES / to MAKE a LEFT-HAND TURN DOWN THERE

Video 2 page 40

when euroPEans / first CAME to ausTRAlia / what they SAW // in THEIR EYES // were JUST these SAVages / LIving on the LAND / and NOT DOing ANYthing WITH it // and in FACT / they MISSED OUT / ON / one of the GREAtest / SUbtle phiLOsophies / of ANY / CULture / on the PLAnet

Video 3 page 58

the Images proVIded by the HUbble SPACE TElescope / conTInue to aSTOnish / AND aMAZE // AND proVIDE a WINdow / on the WONders of SPACE / no MAtter HOW / you SEE them

Video 4 page 76

i would've been surPRISED // NOT to get that FINding // er beCAUSE it's ACtually / VEry conSIStent with what we KNOW from // FINdings in a LOT of er / NON-human SPEcies.

FILE 16

Unit 7 page 63   CONVERSATION PRACTICE

Student B

Article 1

Japanese scientists have made see-through frogs commercially available. The frogs, which are sold for around $100 each, were bred for educational purposes. Rather than getting killed and cut open in class, the transparent frogs now allow students to see internal organs in action.

Researchers in Boston had previously created transparent fish to aid them in their study of the development of cancer. The fish, which are genetically similar to humans, have cancerous cells inserted in their bodies so researchers can watch them grow. Studies on normal animals only show cancer development via medical examinations carried out after death. It is hoped a greater understanding of cancer growth will pave the way for new treatments.

Article 2

A nuclear physicist who had had funding requests for research into time reversal rejected has raised $40,000 from the public to carry out his experiment. Professor John Cramer, a leading scientist in quantum mechanics, is attempting to tackle a famous mystery in quantum theory. Sub-atomic particles that have been split in half can travel faster than the speed of light and 'communicate' directly with each other. It may sound like science fiction, but one theory for this is what has been dubbed 'retrocausality' – in other words, the idea that the future can affect the present or past. Professor Cramer's experiments are seen as a first step towards a full exploration of the theory. If successful, he hopes to attract further funding from government.

FILE 19

Unit 8 page 75   READING

Group B

ONE OF A KIND

The Aye-Aye **resembles a cross between** a small monkey and a rat because of its rodent-like front teeth. It lives in **the canopy of trees** in the Madagascan rainforest, usually nesting in a fork of the tree. As well as fruit and vegetation, it also eats small worms and insects living in the trees, which it finds in a similar way to a woodpecker. It **taps on the trunk** until it detects a hollow 1 sound, then gnaws away at the bark with its teeth to make a hole before inserting its elongated middle finger in through the hole to pull the grubs out. There is only one other animal that uses this technique: the striped possum.

When **foraging for food**, Aye-Ayes may cover over four kilometres a night as they leap from treetop to treetop. Aye-Ayes are generally **solitary creatures** that only socialise in order to mate, with the female of the species being dominant. The males will often aggressively compete for a female's attention.

The Aye-Aye is endangered because of a number of factors. Firstly, its habitat is being destroyed, increasingly forcing it to **raid villages** for food. It is quite fearless in approaching humans, but unfortunately humans are not always friendly towards it. Villagers not only kill Aye-Ayes because they are a nuisance and eat farm crops, but also because they are believed to be evil – capable of **creeping into homes** and puncturing a person's heart while they sleep.

Although laws exist against killing them and several **reserves in the jungle** have been set up, their numbers continue to decline. Captive breeding programmes are also working to preserve them.

FILE 17

Student C

Article 1

Researchers have discovered that autism sufferers who inhale the hormone oxytocin are better at noticing facial signals and maintaining eye contact. The so-called 'love' hormone is found in high levels in breast milk and is thought to be responsible for the development of the special, close relationship between mother and child. Previous studies have also shown those with autistic conditions may have an oxytocin deficiency.

The experiment focused on sufferers who did not have particularly impaired language skills but who struggled with face-to-face contact. Currently, other drugs are prescribed to deal with more visible symptoms such as anxiety, but researchers believe this could be a breakthrough in dealing with the underlying causes of autism.

Article 2

A study by vets in Britain has revealed that, on average, cat owners are more intelligent than dog owners as cat owners typically have a higher level of education. The researchers suggest that this is unlikely to be a result of exposure to the famously independent and cunning pets but rather is due to the fact that cats tend to require less attention and are thus a better fit with busy lifestyles. As highly educated people are likely to work longer hours in more high-powered jobs, they tend not to have the time to look after a dog. This is just one finding of a census undertaken by the Department of Clinical Veterinary Science at the University of Bristol.

FILE 18

Group C

BILBAO

Since its completion in 1997, the Guggenheim Museum in Bilbao, the capital of the Basque region of northern Spain, has become one of the most famous buildings in the world. Many people will have visited the city just to see it and found a flourishing city with a vibrant nightlife. However, fewer will be aware of the profound change that **the gallery symbolises**. Up until the early 80s, Bilbao had been **dominated by steel plants** and shipbuilding, which brought wealth but which also created heavy smog that choked the city. However, during the latter part of that decade, the city was hit by an economic downturn that saw many factories close down and **unemployment soar**. The city was also affected by threats and acts of terrorism by the Basque Separatist group, ETA. Apart from causing problems for local people, all of this also **discouraged inward investment** and tourism to the city. Over the years, many factories closed down and thousands of people **abandoned the city**, leaving contaminated land and large numbers of condemned buildings.

To halt the decline, the city **embarked on a strategy** to reinvent itself as a centre for culture, tourism and new technologies. Obviously, constructing a series of major buildings designed by famous international architects was a key part of this process. However, it's important to recognise it was only *one* part of the strategy. Other cities trying to replicate the so-called 'Guggenheim effect' may have failed because they didn't take up the other strands of Bilbao's regeneration project. These included **ongoing heavy investment** in training and education with a particular focus on computing and technology. The city improved transport links and created two metro lines, and also developed service industries such as **hosting events** and conferences. It also modernised what remained of its more traditional industries and attracted new companies to the technology park on the outskirts of the city.

There have been some **voices of opposition** that suggest the process did not benefit many of the working-class people most affected by the original crisis. Nevertheless, it's difficult to deny it's been a success which has seen the city return to its previous population levels and **survive the major recession** that began in 2008.

AUDIO SCRIPTS

UNIT 1

▶ TRACK 1

1
A: How was your trip?
B: Great. Really amazing. Have you ever been there?
A: No. What's it like?
B: It's really wild. It took me by surprise, actually.
A: Yeah?
B: Yeah. I don't know what I expected, really. I just thought it'd be quieter, but the nightlife is totally insane.
A: Really?
B: Honestly. We went out with these people and ended up in a place at about four in the morning and it was absolutely packed.
A: Yeah?
B: Seriously. You literally couldn't move. In fact, the whole city was still buzzing. You can still get stuck in traffic at that time of night.
A: Wow!
B: Actually, that was a bit of a pain, the congestion.
A: Really? Is it bad?
B: Unbelievable! You just spend hours and hours in the taxi crawling along with everyone sounding their horns. You'd be quicker walking, really.
A: So did you?
B: No, it's unbearably humid, so at least the car has air con. Honestly, you walk out of your hotel and it's like hitting this thick wall of heat. You just die walking in that heat for any length of time.
A: There must be a fair amount of pollution, then.
B: That as well. The smog is incredible. I mean, our hotel was supposed to have this amazing view – and I guess it would be on a clear day – but half the time you can hardly see a thing. And you nearly choke on the fumes when you're outside.
A: Sounds pretty awful. Are you sure it's so great?
B: Well, you know, it does have its drawbacks but, as I say, it just has a real buzz – especially downtown with the skyscrapers and the neon lights flashing and the people and the noise. It's just a really, really vibrant place.

2
C: What's your home town like? It's supposed to be nice, isn't it?
D: It is, if you like that sort of place.
C: What do you mean?
D: It's just very conservative. You know, it's very affluent – you see loads and loads of people in fur coats and posh cars, and the streets are spotless, but it's also just incredibly dull. There's not much going on.
C: Right.
D: I know it's a bit more run-down here, but at least it's more lively. There's more of a music scene, you know.

C: Yeah, I know what you mean. So you wouldn't consider going back to live there?
D: Maybe. I mean, don't get me wrong, it is a good place to live if you're bringing up kids – everything works very smoothly and, as I say, there's not a trace of litter on the streets. So if I were to settle down, I might move back. It's just not what I want right now.
C: Fair enough.

▶ TRACK 2

1
A really terrible thing happened to a woman I used to work with. One day, she woke up and found her car had been stolen from outside her house. So she called the police and reported it, but when she got back home from the office that night, the car had been returned. It was in the driveway. It had been completely cleaned and there was a note on the driver's seat apologising for taking it. Whoever had written the note said that his mum had been taken ill and he'd had to drive her to hospital. Next to the note there were a couple of tickets for a concert the following day. The woman was really thrilled, you know, so happy – her car back, two free tickets, fantastic! So she called a friend and they both went to the concert and had a really fantastic time. Once she got home though, ...

2
Someone told me a story about a guy from Tokyo who'd gone on a golfing holiday. On the third or fourth day, he suddenly collapsed and had to be rushed to hospital for treatment. Eventually, they diagnosed him as having been poisoned and they reported the incident to the police. The detective in charge of the case questioned the man, but he couldn't think of any reason why anybody would want to poison him. It was something really silly in the end. They worked out ...

3
This mad thing happened to a guy that a friend of my brother knows. Apparently, one day he went to a supermarket to buy a few bits and pieces and as he was walking up and down the aisles looking for the bread, he noticed this elderly woman just staring at him with these desperately sad eyes. He turned away, grabbed a loaf and went off in search of some milk. Once he'd found the milk, he turned round only to see the same woman there again – still just staring like mad at him. Anyway, he was getting a bit freaked out by this, as you would, so he rushed off to pay, but then he remembered that he'd run out of toilet paper and so he went back to get some. When he got back to the cashier, there was the old woman again – in front of him in the queue and her trolley was almost full to the brim. This time she turns to him and she says, 'I'm really sorry for staring, but the thing is, you're the spitting image of my son who died last year.' She's wiping her eyes, getting all tearful, and she says, 'You've got the same eyes, the same hair. It's incredible.' As she was packing all her stuff away, she whispered to the guy and said, 'Could you do me a tiny little favour? Could you just say "Goodbye, Mum" when I leave? It'd mean the world to me.' Well,

what was he going to do? This little old lady and her tragic story, trying to hold back the tears. So, as she's leaving the store, struggling with all her shopping, he shouts out, 'Goodbye Mum.' He felt like he'd done his good deed for the day, but then ...

▶ TRACK 3

1
Once she got home though, she discovered she'd been burgled and all her valuables had been stolen. Then, to top that, about a week later, the police called her and told her that her car had been used as the vehicle to get away from a major bank robbery on the day that it had gone missing. That is so unlucky, no?

2
It was something really silly in the end. They worked out that the man had actually poisoned himself by accident. Apparently, when he was playing golf he used to hold the tee – that plastic thing you put the golf ball on – between his teeth as he was walking round between the holes, but the golf course had been sprayed with pesticide, so he was basically just sucking in toxic pesticide.

3
He felt like he'd done his good deed for the day, but then the cashier told him his bill was like £300. He said there must've been a mistake as he'd only bought a few things, but then the cashier explained. She said, 'Yes, I know, but your mother said you'd pay for all her shopping as well!'

UNIT 2

▶ TRACK 4

1
A: So how's it all going? Any better?
B: I'd say things are worse if anything, to be honest. He doesn't seem to have a clue how the department should work or what's expected of him and he's dragging the whole team down with him. I've tried to talk to him about it, but he always just gets really defensive and puts up this great big barrier and basically just tells me to get on with my work. What really drives me mad, though, is the man's arrogance. He's so full of himself! He's one of those people who'll just never accept they've made the wrong decision. He just blames it all on everyone else – mainly those below him.
A: Sounds like an idiot to me! Maybe you need to go over his head and talk to his line manager about it.
B: Oh, it's not worth it. He isn't exactly the most approachable person and from what I've heard he wouldn't take any notice, anyway. They seem oblivious to criticism, these people. All they're interested in is sucking up to whoever is above them in order to get ahead.

2
C: I can't stand him.
D: Really? I've always thought he comes across as a really decent guy.

C: You're joking, aren't you? He's so fake!

D: D'you think so? In what way?

C: All that rubbish about saving the world and helping the starving millions that he's always going on about.

D: What's wrong with that? I quite admire the fact that he's prepared to stand up for what he believes in. There are plenty of people in the public eye who just aren't bothered about those things. It'd be easier for him to just keep his mouth shut.

C: I wouldn't say that. I'd say it's all just self-promotion. It's just to sell more of his music. If he was really bothered, he'd give his millions away and really help people. He just likes to be seen to be doing good.

D: I just think you've got him wrong. He's done a lot to raise awareness of various different causes and he works really hard to make a difference. You're just a cynic.

C: And you're just naïve!

3

E: So what're the people on your corridor like? Are you getting on OK with them all?

F: Yeah, more or less. I haven't really seen much of the guy next door. I think he studies Medicine so he's either at lectures or studying. He certainly keeps himself to himself, anyway.

E: OK.

F: But the girl opposite is great. She's really nice and very bright and chatty. We hit it off straight away.

E: That's good, then.

F: Yeah, she's from the States and came over to do a Master's in International Law.

E: Really? So she's a bit older than you, then.

F: Yeah, but she certainly doesn't make a thing of it. She's a great laugh. The only problem is she kind of takes over the bathroom every morning. She's in there for hours doing her hair and her make-up. It's really annoying because we've only got the one bathroom.

E: Oh no! Really? That'd drive me mad, that would!

F: And the guy on the other side of me seems pleasant enough, but he strikes me as a bit of a slacker. I mean, I see him throwing a frisbee around with people outside the hall or sitting around smoking, but I've never seen him go to any lectures or anything, and he just seems ... well ... extremely laid-back about it.

E: To the point of horizontal, then, eh?

▶ TRACK 5

1 The new restrictions? Oh, they brought them in last year.

2 He's not just messing up his own career. He's dragging us down as well.

3 We realised as soon as we embarked on it that it was a good strategy.

4 He made millions, but then gave it all away.

5 Life brings many changes – and I've gone through them all!

6 The buildings aren't fit to live in anymore so they've decided to knock them down.

7 It's quite an ambitious plan, so make sure you set it out clearly.

8 There's a big recycling centre there. They set it up a few years ago.

9 If those are your principles, you've got to stick to them.

10 I can never get in the bathroom in the morning. She totally takes it over.

▶ TRACK 6

1

When he was a toddler, I'd do the childcare most days and he was always a bit of a handful. I did try and instil a bit of discipline into him, but I'm not sure it really happened at home. My son would shout and tell him off, but then he'd burst into tears and his mother would comfort him, so totally mixed messages. I knew it would come to no good, but you can't really interfere, can you? Not that he's all bad. He's helped me out sometimes since I've been unsteady on me feet. But really, if it's true, I hope they treat him severely. It's what he needs to get back on the straight and narrow.

2

The frustrating thing is he's a bright lad, but I would say he has a stubborn streak and he's been prone to outbursts and answering back. I remember once I asked him to change desks to sit next to this girl and he just wouldn't – just refused point blank – and then we got into this ridiculous confrontation with neither of us willing to back down. I had to call the Head in the end. So yeah, I guess it doesn't entirely surprise me he's ended up in this kind of trouble. What should happen now? Well, he should obviously be punished, but after that I'd still give him another chance rather than exclude him permanently. I'm sure he'll learn.

3

Oh yeah, hugely talented and I would've thought he could go all the way and turn professional, so this has come as a big shock. Maybe there's more to it than appears to be the case. He certainly conducted himself well here. You know, I push them hard, but he's just taken that in his stride and done everything I've asked of him. He's had the odd dispute on the pitch, but I always took that to be part of the game rather than something particular to him. He confided that his parents were going through a rough patch and I was aware that he had a few issues at school, but I think training and matches were always an escape from that and I made sure he was always focused. Hopefully, this is just a setback rather than the end of his career prospects.

4

I've been treating him since he came in here. He suffered some quite severe blows, but the operation went very well. It helped he was in remarkably good health for someone of his age and although he's a little frail now, I'd expect him to make a complete recovery. We're going to monitor him for a few more days, but we'll probably discharge him next week. From what I understand, he's still a bit confused about what happened, but he seems to think the young man who was arrested had actually come to his aid.

5

He's in my class and we kinda went out for a while. He can turn on the charm and that, but he was just too unreliable. When it came down to it, the only thing he was committed to was his football. We'd arrange something, but then he'd be like, 'Oh, the coach wants to put us through our paces', or 'Coach says we're getting complacent, gotta stay on', 'Early night. Coach says I've gotta conserve my energy for the game.' Tch! I said, 'You might as well go out with Coach cos you've let me down too often!' I probably would've stayed with him if he'd apologised, but he's too proud, inne. Just walked away. It was cold. It's been awkward in class. I actually saw him the night it happened at this friend's party. I don't know what was up with him. He was acting strangely – staring at the people I was with – and there was, like, a bit of a scene, but I still doubt he'd do something like that.

UNIT 3

▶ TRACK 7

1

C = Chrissy, Z = Zoe

C: Zoe! I'm over here.

Z: Chrissy. How are you? You're looking great!

C: Thanks, so are you. I like that top.

Z: Yeah, it's nice, isn't it? Mehdi got it for me.

C: Very good taste. How is he?

Z: Oh ... he's OK. A bit down.

C: Really? Fed up with the miserable winter?

Z: No, no, not really. It's the people that he seems to be struggling with.

C: Oh?

Z: Yeah, apparently he's sick of our British hypocrisy!

C: Oof, that's a bit harsh, isn't it? It's not as though everyone's like that.

Z: Mmm, I have pointed that out ...

C: Oh, so what's brought that on? Doesn't sound like him.

Z: It's not and I try not to take it personally. It's really more about his work.

C: Oh? Not paying him enough?

Z: Well, that too probably. No, what he hates is all the bitchy comments and gossip.

C: Really? He's not just misinterpreting it? You know, people sometimes just take the mickey and don't mean things to be taken seriously.

Z: Yeah, I know it can be like that sometimes here, and they are more formal where he's from – at least in the work setting.

C: Mmm.

Z: Then again, it might not be the usual jokes.

C: Right.

Z: And I guess the bottom line is that he's just not like that and it makes it difficult to fit in.

C: Tch, oh, that's not good.

Z: No. I mean, people are polite to him, but he just feels it's a bit superficial and that he's always going to be an outsider.

C: Aww, that's such a shame. He's such a lovely bloke.

2

A: How did it go?

B: Oh man, the bureaucracy here! It just drives me insane. We're in the 21st century! You should be able to do everything online rather than doing it in person.

A: I know. Mind you, the thing that really frustrates me is the fact that they only ever seem to have one person serving you.

B: Yeah, yeah. When I went this morning ... it wasn't that they were short-staffed. There were plenty of others in the rest of the office, but all they did was stare at their computer screens or file papers.

A: I know! And when I went to get a parking permit, there was a queue of about 100 people even before the place opened, but they only had two people actually dealing with them all.

B: Oh, tell me about it!

A: Still, people were very funny about it, in that dry, understated way they have here, you know, which I guess is the best outlook to have.

B: Yeah, but then again, how will anything ever change?

3

C: So, how did you find it?

D: Really, really amazing.

C: Yeah, the people there are so welcoming – and the hospitality!

D: I know! I was invited into people's homes or offered tea or dinner so many times.

C: Absolutely. And the other thing I loved about it was the fact that they've managed to maintain their culture and traditions.

D: I guess.

C: You don't think?

D: Yeah, but the flip side is it must be difficult if you don't conform.

C: Mmm, I suppose so.

D: And women are still looked down on and have fewer rights.

C: I'm not sure about that. Just because most take on that traditional home-building role, it doesn't mean they're looked down on, does it?

D: No, of course not, but what I heard from people there is that with the economy developing, more women are starting to study and even work now, and it's the women who are pushing the government to do more to break down barriers. So, you know, there's still a fair way to go.

C: Oh, right, OK. I hadn't grasped all that.

▶ TRACK 8

1   Savannah

I grew up in London, which is incredibly multicultural, so my feelings about British culture have obviously been influenced by that. Half my friends were mixed race like me and we all grew up going to the Notting Hill Carnival, eating curry and kebabs, listening to Jamaican music, American music. You know, a real mixed bag of stuff. Now, though, I live in Lincolnshire, which is much more what you might call traditionally English. It's much whiter, for a start! I'm enjoying it, though, I have to say. I love the countryside up here and the big, empty skies, and I love all the local car boot sales as well. I've picked up some mad stuff there. I've started gardening too and getting into baking, which is a whole new thing for me. My London friends would die laughing if they could see me now!

2   Callum

One thing that bugs me is people talking about 'British' culture when what they really mean, whether they're aware of it or not, is English! Scotland's a separate country with its own distinct cultural heritage. Politically, we're more left wing, but that's not reflected in the British government, which is still dominated by these southern English public school boys.

We're more in control of what goes on up here than we used to, but personally I'd like even more autonomy – and maybe one day independence! Also, I don't understand why we still cling on to the Royal Family. The only 'God Save the Queen' I'll sing along to is an old anti-royalist punk song! In some ways, I'd like to be seen as a republican and a citizen of the world first, then European and Scottish, or even British – but never English!

3   Amir

Some people might not expect someone like me to be running a fish and chip shop, but for most of me customers it's just not an issue. I was born here as were my parents and I'm as British as anyone else. I just happen to be Muslim as well, that's all. It's no big thing. I mean, it's not exactly unusual nowadays, is it? I do get the occasional comment about it, but I don't let it bother me.

The only time I ever feel vaguely conflicted about my identity is when England play Pakistan at cricket. I can't help it, but I always want Pakistan to do well. There's generally a bit of friendly joking about that with the local lads, but, as I always say, I'm sure most English blokes who end up moving to Spain still want their kids to support the English football team. It's human nature, isn't it?

▶ TRACK 9

1   It's really no big thing.
2   It's just not the done thing.
3   chance would be a fine thing
4   It's the furthest thing from my mind.
5   first thing in the morning
6   It's the sort of thing that makes you glad to be alive.
7   what with one thing and another
8   One thing just led to another.

▶ TRACK 10

As you're no doubt all aware, we live in troubled times, and one reaction to global uncertainty has always been to cling onto this idea of a unified national culture, a culture that everyone living in a particular land shares and participates in. It's an idea that many find very comforting. Sadly, though, I'm afraid it's also something of a myth.

The reality is that identity is a very personal thing, and the individual cultural identities of people living in pretty much any society that you care to name vary so much that it's basically impossible to define common features. And of course, our identities aren't fixed or static. They change over time as a result of our interactions. And in an increasingly globalised world, a world that's driven by commerce, our interactions are becoming more and more complex and multi-layered.

We can easily find ourselves eating a breakfast that's been manufactured by a Swiss company while watching a French TV show we recorded last night on our Korean-made TV. We might then put on a Chinese-produced T-shirt, some American-made jeans and some Italian shoes before getting into a German-made car to drive to work. I should know – that's exactly what I did this morning!

If our habits as consumers complicate our ideas about what it means to belong to a national culture, then so too do our relationships with others. As we get older, we often grow into the many distinct roles we play in life. These different roles often exist independently of each other and when playing a particular role, we sometimes end up only interacting with those directly affected by whatever the role is. This is why it's quite possible for one person to be, for instance, a mother, a wife, a ballet lover, Welsh, British, Jamaican, black, and a marketing manager – without any contradiction.

At the same time, though, we also need to realise that for some people these different roles can cause terrible tensions and can result in individuals abandoning certain roles as they feel they're no longer compatible with the main ways in which they have come to see themselves. I'm sure you can all think of examples of this kind of thing from your own experience of the world.

So where does all of this leave national identity? The historian Eric Hobsbawm has argued that many of the ideas about national cultures that are spread through the education system, through the media, and through public ceremonies and monuments are basically a form of myth-making – and it's the ruling elite who encourage these stories and, of course, who benefit.

UNIT 4

▶ TRACK 11

1

A: I don't know about you, but personally I'm in favour of limiting the salaries of people like bankers and executives.

B: Yeah? Really? How would you do that, though?

A: I don't know. I'm sure it's not without problems, but something's got to be done. Honestly, I just think some of these salaries are obscene – especially when there are people in the same company who you know are earning peanuts.

B: Mmm, yeah. I do know what you mean.

A: And it just distorts everything else because if they're earning that much, it encourages other people to ask for more, and it all just pushes up prices.

B: Mmm, restricting salaries may be OK in principle, but in practice? I mean, even if they do manage to introduce this new law, it's basically going to be unworkable, isn't it?

A: I don't see why. We have a minimum wage so why not a maximum one? The bottom line is that as long as there's the official desire to make it work, then it'll work.

B: Maybe, I guess. So how would this maximum amount be decided? And what would you include in pay? Supposing they were given a boat, or whatever, instead of money?

A: Well, they'd just declare it as part of their income in the normal way, no? And it could be, say, ten times the lowest wage.

B: Only ten? I'm sure they'd be able to find ways round it. And you don't think it'd discourage people from doing those jobs?

A: Some, maybe, but I don't see that as a bad thing. I mean, maybe they'd think about doing other jobs that are more useful. Anyway, I thought you said it was a good idea in theory.

B: I did. I'm just playing devil's advocate. But, as I said, I do have major doubts about how it'd work.

A: Well, personally, I think the benefits far outweigh the difficulties.

2

C: Did you hear about this proposal to bid to hold the Olympics here?

D: Yeah. You don't sound too happy about it.

C: No, absolutely not! I'm totally opposed to it. It's a complete waste of money. Aren't you against it?

D: I'm not really sure where I stand on it, to be honest. Won't the Games make a lot of money if we get them?

C: No! They always talk about them leaving a good legacy and boosting the economy, but it's all rubbish.

D: Really? I can't pass judgement. I don't know enough about it.

C: Doh! Have a look on the Internet. I mean, take Montreal, for example. The Olympics were held there way back in 1976 and the city then took another 30 years to clear off the debt the whole thing created!

D: Seriously?

C: I'm telling you! It's lucky we don't have a hope in hell, so they'll only waste the money on the bid. Imagine if we actually won it, though! It'd be a recipe for disaster. It'd probably bankrupt us!

▶ TRACK 12

A politician has died and has arrived at the gates of heaven **clutching** his bags. The gatekeeper stops him and says, 'Don't make up your mind just yet. Try out hell and heaven first and see what you think.' The politician **hops** in the lift down to hell and when he gets out he finds he's in an incredible seven-star hotel. Many of his old friends are lounging round the huge pool, sipping expensive drinks and **chattering** to each other. When they see him, they all **cheer** 'Hello!' and welcome him over. Later in the day, he **strolls** round the fantastic golf course with his best friend and scores his lowest score ever. Later in the evening, there's a huge party and he dances the night away.

The following day, he goes back to heaven with the music and laughter ringing in his ears. He **steps** into heaven and into a lovely restaurant overlooking a beautiful beach. There is soft classical music and the murmur of gentle conversation. After his meal, he **strolls** along the beach and **gazes** at the beautiful sunset. He returns to his hotel and settles into his super-comfy bed and falls fast asleep.

In the morning, he goes to the gatekeeper who asks him, 'So, what d'you think? Have you decided?' And the politician says, 'You know, don't get me wrong, heaven was great – all very relaxing and lovely – but, I have to say, I would never have imagined that hell could be so much fun.' So, he waves goodbye and happily **skips** into the lift to take him down to hell.

When the doors open, though, he is faced with a scene of devastation. It's like there's been an earthquake, or something. He **peers** into the distance and **spots** some people on the horizon. As he walks towards them, he sees that they are his friends **trudging** along under the weight of heavy rocks while the devil **yells**, 'Work harder!' Some are **crawling** on the floor in exhaustion and hunger. The politician goes up to the devil and **gasps**, 'But what are you doing? What's happened? Where's the hotel? The golf? The party?'

The devil **chuckles** and shakes his head. 'Oh dear, you should know. That was the election campaign and now you've voted!

▶ TRACK 13

1
I used to like watching *Star Quality*, but since this scandal has erupted I've lost interest in it. This story leaked out that they were encouraging people to phone in even though they'd already decided the result. They were manipulating things so that one guy didn't get

voted off because it helped the programme's ratings if they had a kind of hate figure. I might not have minded so much if the calls were free, but they're making a fortune on them.

2
We only called a vote because negotiations were going absolutely nowhere and, despite the massive support we've received from our members, the management is persisting with a ridiculous offer that will basically result in a drop in the value of wages next year. If they hadn't been so reluctant to negotiate, we would not be taking this action now. We understand the public's anger and frustration – we share it – but the blame for this dispute lies firmly with the train company, not with us.

3
I'm totally in favour of a vote on the issue. The way the current system works, some parties get a seat with only 100,000 votes, while others who poll more than twice that don't get any. In the run-up to the election, the New Party had promised to hold one if they got into power, but in the event all that talk has faded away. I guess if they hadn't won a landslide victory, they'd be keener to bring about electoral reform, but I truly believe the vast majority of the electorate still wants to see a change and would vote yes, whatever their reservations.

4
To be honest, I suspect that if they'd called on another day, I wouldn't have taken part, but I was at a bit of a loose end when the researcher called and so had some time to spare. It took about half an hour, and I have to admit I quite enjoyed it – moaning about the government! Mind you, when the results were published in the paper, I was a bit taken aback. It seems I'm in a small minority. People must be mad!

5
It's easy to be cynical and to say that it changes nothing – that it's all just done to create the illusion of fairness and inclusivity – but I can assure you that simply isn't the case here. Given that relatively few people vote these days, we feel it's essential for young people to learn that democracy can contribute to positive change. Apart from deciding things like the end-of-term trips, pupil reps can also decide on policy. It's unlikely we would've abolished uniforms if we didn't have a body like this. It isn't compulsory to vote, but nearly everyone does.

UNIT 5

▶ TRACK 14

1
A: Hey, Maddy. You're in late today. Are you OK? You look tired.

B: I am. I'm exhausted. I didn't crawl home till almost three.

A: Yeah? How come?

B: Oh, this friend of mine … it was her 25th and we'd organised a surprise party.

A: Oh, that's nice. I bet she was pleased.

B: Yeah, she was, although she actually burst into tears when she first came in.

A: Oh no!

B: Yeah. She's been through a lot recently, which is partly why we'd planned the do.

A: Cheer her up?

B: Yeah, exactly. Anyway, she was clearly a bit overwhelmed by it all at first, but she soon got over it.

A: Oh, well, that's good. Where was it?

B: In this bar in town. We hired a room and managed to book this band who were friends of hers.

A: Oh really? Were they any good?

B: Yeah, brilliant. They do this kind of old school rock and roll stuff and they went down really, really well. Honestly, everyone was up dancing.

A: Was Marco there?

B: But of course! Giving it his all on the dance floor as usual.

A: Ah, he's so full of himself, that guy. He thinks he's God's gift to women!

B: Oh, that's a bit harsh. He seems pretty harmless to me. He just loves a good dance.

A: Yeah? Well, it could just be me, I suppose. Glad he behaved himself, anyway.

B: Yeah. Hey, talking of dancing, are you still going to those tango classes?

A: Yeah, on and off.

B: You must be getting quite good, then.

A: I wouldn't go that far. I'm still a bit prone to treading on toes.

2
C: Oh, Almir. Hi. I'm glad I caught you. I just wanted to check whether you've managed to sort everything out for the big meeting yet.

D: Yup. It's all in hand – and I've also booked a table at St John's for the evening.

C: That sounds perfect. I didn't mean to hassle you. I'm just stressing about it.

D: That's all right. I'm sure it'll all be fine.

C: Yeah, of course it will. It's just that I could do without it at the moment. I've got far too much on.

D: I can imagine. Anyway, as I said, it's all under control.

C: That's great. Thanks for being so on top of things.

D: No problem at all.

C: Oh, by the way, how was your meal the other night?

D: It was great, thanks. We went to this new place, Porchetta?

C: Oh yeah. How was the food?

D: Amazing, but there was so much of it! They do something like six or seven courses. I lost count after a while.

C: That must've been quite filling.

D: It was. I was ready to burst by the end of it all! It was a bit too much, to be honest.

C: Mmm.

D Actually, I almost forgot … there was a bit of a scene while we were there.

C: Oh?

D: Yeah. This guy at a table in the corner just suddenly burst out screaming at one of the waiters.

C: Really? How come?

D: I'm not sure, actually. I didn't catch it all, but it was about something daft – like a dirty fork, or something.

C: Strange!

D: I know. There was a kind of awkward silence in the room while it was all going on.

C: I bet. That can't have been much fun.

D: Mmm.

Audio scripts **105**

C: So what happened in the end, then?

D: Oh, they managed to get him to leave. But otherwise, yeah, it was good.

▶ TRACK 15

1 A: That must've been pretty dull.
  B: Awful! I couldn't stop yawning.

2 A: You can't be feeling your best at the moment.
  B: Actually, I feel surprisingly fresh.

3 A: He can't have been very pleased when he found out.
  B: You can say that again! He went totally mental!

4 A: You must be glad you didn't go now.
  B: Absolutely! It obviously didn't live up to the hype.

5 A: That can't have been cheap.
  B: You'd be surprised, actually. It wasn't as pricey as you'd think.

6 A: She must've been feeling quite unwell.
  B: Yeah, I guess so. I mean, she's usually the last person to leave, isn't she?

7 A: Judging from his accent, he can't be from here.
  B: No, I know. He sounds Australian or something, I thought.

8 A: You must be joking!
  B: No, honestly! I'm deadly serious.

▶ TRACK 16

P = Presenter, B = Bryan Sewer

P: For several years now, Mark Zuckerberg, the billionaire co-founder of Facebook, has been making very public – and often quite eccentric – New Year's resolutions. There was the year he promised to only eat meat that he'd killed himself and the time he vowed to learn Mandarin Chinese; then there was the year when he tried to meet a different new person who wasn't an employee every single day. And then in 2015, he announced he'd be switching his media diet towards reading more books. He planned to get through one every fortnight. To aid him in this pursuit, he set up a page called *A Year of Books* on his own social networking site, where recommendations could be dissected and discussed. Its impact was both dramatic and immediate.

With its focus on learning about different cultures, beliefs, histories and technologies, the page soon had half a million followers, and was making a huge difference to sales of selected titles. Purchases of *The End Of Power* by Venezuelan journalist Moisés Naím rocketed after it was chosen as the first title for consideration, with the book jumping to the top of Amazon's economics chart overnight!

The degree to which Zuckerberg will continue to influence popular purchases remains to be seen, but the venture is very much in keeping with broader cultural trends. Social media has had a marked influence on reading choices over recent years, with, for instance, tens of thousands sharing current enthusiasms on Twitter, using hashtags like 'amreading' or 'fridayreads'. We are also seeing what UNESCO has dubbed 'a mobile reading revolution' across the developing world, where in the past paper-based products were hard to come by. Now though, according to one recent survey, 62% read

more as they can freely access books on their phones. This has resulted in initiatives such as the Africa-wide cell phone book club, started by a Zimbabwean librarian.

Of course, all this online activity is an extension of the face-to-face reading groups which have thrived since the start of the century. If you'd googled the phrase 'book club' back in 2003, it would've returned around 400,000 hits; try it today and you're guaranteed more than 30 million! In Britain alone, there are now an estimated 40,000 reading groups, with people meeting to discuss their latest literary loves in private homes or cafés, in libraries and in bookstores. This phenomenon has resulted in specialist gatherings, such as a Vegan Book Club and a Socialist Feminist group, as well as meetings specifically targeted at lovers of crime novels and even comics! Now, let's say each club has around ten members, and picks perhaps six books a year, then that's 60 books per club and almost two and a half million sales per year. And that's before you even factor in the power of Facebook! Not everyone, though, sees these trends in such a positive light. Here's literary critic Bryan Sewer:

S: Let's face it, most reading groups are little more than gossiping circles, or else simply a literary guise for dating clubs! I know from my own observations that when members do finally get round to discussing books, the discourse is generally basic and displays limited insight or intelligence. I also suspect that these groups consume far too much sentimental autobiographical writing. One can only assume it must be easier for a mass audience to digest.

P: Such opinions, though, seem to have had little impact and certainly haven't halted the spread of communal reading. Indeed, one book club favourite, *Reading Lolita in Tehran* by Azar Nafisi, details the impact that the experience of reading and discussing frequently banned Western books in the Iranian capital in the 1990s had on the lives of eight young women. The appeal, it would seem, is universal.

UNIT 6

▶ TRACK 17

1

A: Argh!

B: What've you broken? Oh my word! What a mess!

A: Don't!

B: OK! Calm down! It's not the end of the world!

A: Don't tell me to calm down. If only you'd put things away properly!

B: I'm sorry?

A: That is your bag, isn't it?

B: Oh ... yeah, I was going to take it to my room ...

A: Well, I wish you had. I almost broke my neck!

B: OK. Sorry. It's not as though I did it deliberately.

A: That's not the point. You're constantly leaving your stuff lying around. You know, I'm not your mother to clear up after you.

B: Right, of course – Mr Perfect!

A: Come on! That's not what I'm saying!

B: Well, that's what it sounds like. It's not as if you're the only one who does stuff round the house.

A: Yeah. OK. Whatever. Listen, forget it. I wish I hadn't said anything.

B: No, if that's how you really feel ...

A: No, it came out wrong. I'm sorry. It's just that it's been a long day and this was the last straw.

B: OK. Well, I am sorry. I will make an effort, although in this particular case I went to answer a phone call and then I forgot about it.

A: Whatever. It's done. Can we just move on?

B: OK. Can I give you a hand?

A: Yeah. Can you grab the dustpan and brush?

2

C: Miriam, could I have a word?

D: Erm, could we not talk later? I'm actually in a bit of a hurry, as it happens.

C: I'd rather not leave it.

D: Oh, OK. What's wrong?

C: Listen. I just had a phone call from that group who were coming in July and they're cancelling.

D: What? You're joking?

C: I wish I was. Apparently, they were unhappy with the service they were getting.

D: What? They haven't even been in touch recently. I assumed everything was fine.

C: They said they'd asked about discounts, but you hadn't got back to them.

D: Er ... yes, but I passed that on to you.

C: When?

D: A couple of weeks ago! I assumed you'd dealt with it.

C: Why? Didn't you even reply to them?

D: No.

C: Or think to bring it to my attention?

D: Well, you were the one who said you wanted to take control of everything.

C: What? When?

D: Last month – in the departmental meeting.

C: What? That's not what I said at all.

D: You said, 'We've got to get a grip of costs' and that everything had to go through you.

C: That was different.

D: Really? You kind of left us feeling as if we were doing it all wrong and it was as though we'd been wasting money left, right and centre.

C: Really? That certainly wasn't my intention. I wish you'd said something sooner.

D: I would have, but you hardly come out of that office.

C: Well, it's just that I have a tremendous amount on.

D: We actually understand that, but try to see it from our point of view. We want to help, but how can we if you don't communicate more with us?

C: I send out a weekly update.

D: OK, no offence, but that's not exactly the most human thing. I'm not saying it's not helpful – it's just that we'd all appreciate a bit more face-to-face contact.

C: OK, I hear you. And I can see we've got our wires crossed.

D: That's OK, I should've followed up the email. I was probably being a bit petulant, for which I apologise.

C: OK. Well, it's done now. I'm glad we've cleared the air.

D: Is it worth getting back to them?

C: No, I've spoken to them already. Let's just move on. There's no point crying over spilt milk.

▶ TRACK 18

1

A manager of the soft drinks company Jazz Drinks is standing trial today accused of spying for its biggest rival, Pit-Pots. Dan Craddock, a high-level manager at Jazz, is said to have sold crucial strategic information to Pit-Pots for over two million dollars. Over recent years, the two companies have been engaged in a fierce battle to capture market share, pouring money into ever more extravagant advertising campaigns. Last year was Jazz Drinks' best ever and as Pit-Pots was losing ground, it is claimed they secretly recruited Mr Craddock, a sales director at Jazz, to pass on information on marketing and pricing strategy for the coming year. Mr Craddock denies the charges. The case continues.

2

The TV presenter Jonas Bakeman is fighting to save his career after stories appeared of his affair with a researcher on his programme, *Justice Fight*. As reporters laid siege outside his home, he released a statement expressing regret over the affair, but defended himself against allegations that he'd initiated it after aggressively pursuing the woman, Petra Campbell. He claimed the affair had been brief and he had simply surrendered to a foolish moment of weakness at a production party. However, Ms Campbell has made available evidence that she had been bombarded with emails and text messages of a personal nature, and that the affair had been far from 'brief'. Bosses of the TV company are to meet tomorrow to consider Mr Bakeman's future.

3

Campaigners have claimed victory in their battle against full-body scanners in airports following a court decision supporting a woman who refused to accept a scan. A number of civil liberties groups had joined forces to back the woman in an attempt to defeat the government's proposals that everyone travelling by plane should have to pass through the machines. The campaigners say it is a gross invasion of privacy as the scanners can see through clothing. The government has said that it will not retreat in its policy and believes the scanners play a crucial role in protecting the public from terrorism. It plans to appeal against the decision.

4

And finally, peace has now broken out in the village of Paulston. A dispute had been raging over a statue of St John of Bidshire, the multi-prize-winning pig of local farmer Tim Langford. The three-metre pink sculpture, which had been standing at the entrance of the village for over a year, had split the village, with half saying it was hideous, while supporters of Mr Langford said it stood as a proud symbol of the local produce for which Paulston is famous. Protesters had marched onto Mr Langford's land and sprayed the statue with paint. There were then revenge attacks against the vandals. Now the local council has stepped in as peacemaker to solve the dispute. Mr Langford has agreed to the statue being relocated to a nearby sculpture gallery, but it will be moved back to the village during the three-day summer festival.

▶ TRACK 19

1 The two companies have been engaged in a fierce battle to capture market share.

2 ... to pass on information on marketing and pricing strategy for the coming year.

3 He released a statement expressing regret over the affair.

4 She had been bombarded with emails and text messages of a personal nature.

5 Campaigners have claimed victory in their battle against full-body scanners in airports.

6 The scanners play a crucial role in protecting the public from terrorism.

7 ... a statue of St John of Bidshire, the multi-prize-winning pig of local farmer Tim Langford.

8 It stood as a proud symbol of the local produce for which Paulston is famous.

UNIT 7

▶ TRACK 20

1

A: Did you read that thing about transplanting the noses of mosquitoes?

B: What? Are you serious? I didn't think mosquitoes even had noses!

A: Yeah, well, it's obviously not a nose in the sense of our noses, but apparently it's like the smelling receptors on the antennae on their heads. And what they do is they somehow get these receptors to grow inside frog's eggs so that they can do tests on them.

B: How on earth do they do that?

A: To be perfectly honest, I'm not really sure. They extract the DNA from the receptors, or something, and then insert it into the eggs. It's a bit beyond me, really. I just thought it was amazing.

B: It sounds a bit peculiar, if you ask me. I mean, what's the point?

A: Well, apparently, they use them to see what smells trigger the receptors.

B: And?

A: Well, it's to stop the spread of malaria. Obviously, mosquitoes are strongly attracted to the smell of human sweat, but if they can find smells which create a bigger stimulus or which produce no trigger, then they could use those smells to manufacture traps to tempt the mosquitoes away from humans, or spray-on repellents that mask human smells.

B: OK. I suppose that makes sense. I have to say, though, I still find all that gene manipulation a bit worrying.

A: What d'you mean?

B: Well, it's a slippery slope, isn't it? One moment it's mosquito noses, the next they'll be engineering babies.

A: Come off it! It's hardly the same thing!

2

C: Did you read that thing about building a sun shield in space to prevent global warming?

D: No. It sounds a bit unlikely, though. I mean, how big would it have to be?

C: Well, apparently, about 60,000 miles long!

D: 60,000! That's ridiculous! I mean, how on earth are they going to build something that big, let alone get it up there? They struggle to build a stadium here on time and on budget.

C: Well, that's it – the idea with this is it's not like one big structure; it's millions of little reflectors which form a massive 'cloud'.

D: But how many would you need?

C: Trillions. They reckon if they launched a pile of these things every five minutes or so, it'd take ten years to make.

D: Hardly an instant solution, then!

C: No.

D: And what about the cost?

C: I've no idea, to be honest, but they claim it's all quite possible. Anyway, this guy got a grant to look into it further.

D: You're joking! What a waste of money! Are you sure it isn't just a scam or some made-up story?

C: It was on a fairly reliable website. They wouldn't have just made it up.

D: Pah! Mind you, I sometimes wonder whether the whole climate change thing isn't all just a scam. I mean, there are a lot of rich and powerful people out there who stand to benefit from us being scared into believing it's all true.

C: You're not serious, are you?

D: Yeah, why not?

C: Because the evidence is pretty conclusive.

D: Says who?

▶ TRACK 21

1 What on earth for?

2 Why on earth would they want to do that?

3 What on earth's that?

4 Who on earth would buy something like that?

5 Where on earth are they going to get the money for that?

6 What on earth is he going on about?

▶ TRACK 22

P = Presenter, T = Tom Hunter

P: So next, statistics – often thought to be the worst kind of lying there is! A recent survey found that 60% of Britons believe the probability of tossing a coin twice and getting two heads is 50%, rather than the correct answer of 25%. Our guest today, Tom Hunter, thinks this is a worry and says we need to get to grips with stats. Tom, welcome.

T: Hi.

P: So, what's the problem? We don't really make use of stats and probabilities in our daily lives, do we?

T: Oh my! Well, that's a common belief, but gosh! I mean, we're surrounded by statistics: opinion polls, crime figures, product claims in advertising ...

P: Exactly! I mean, it's just used to sell stuff and so we ignore it!

T: Well, of course, statistics can be used to manipulate, but they also inform policy development, scientific progress and many individual decisions. The heart of the matter is that there are good statistics and bad ones. And knowing the difference is empowering.

P: OK. So, how can we tell the good from the bad?

T: Well, we need to recognise that different approaches to data collection have different degrees of validity. And we need to look for underlying problems with any research we encounter.

P: For example?

T: Well, say a food company is having some research done to see if its product has health benefits, right? It has a vested interest in the process, so researchers may get pressured into finding positive results. They may worry about not being employed again, which may affect their conclusions. Similarly, asking 50 people on social media will be less valid than a survey of 5,000 people chosen at random. That's not just because the sample size is too small, but also because social media will tend to attract people of similar views, so this grouping affect may exaggerate the results further.

P: Shouldn't publishers filter out this poor research?

T: Mmm, you'd hope so. Obviously, research in a respected journal, reviewed by other experts, will be better than something published anonymously online, but even peer reviews can underestimate aspects like sample size. And interpretations can also be wrong. So, we always need to be on our guard.

P: Yeah, you mean the wrong conclusions may be drawn, whatever the data?

T: Absolutely. Take the issue of relative and absolute figures.

P: Relative and absolute?

T: Yeah. Say Company A produced 10,000 units last year and increased it to 12,000 this year. That'd be a 20% rise relative to its previous performance and an absolute increase of 2,000 units. Company B, on the other hand, produced 1,000 units last year and 1,400 this year – a rise of 40%. So, by comparing the relative changes, Company B could say it performed twice as well as its rival, but in absolute terms its rival produced an extra 1,600 units compared to Company B.

P: I see.

T: But what's more, Company B may have employed more people to get its increase, while Company A may have achieved theirs whilst cutting staff. So, far from doing 100% better than a rival, Company B's actually being hugely outperformed. And, of course, one year doesn't make a trend. It could just be an anomaly.

P: Maybe they had one client who ordered a huge amount and won't repeat it.

T: Exactly. So you can see it's the focus on either a relative or absolute figure and choosing the start and end point for the figures that can be used to twist data to suit your own ends.

P: Sure. So, what about the probabilities we started with?

T: Well, the initial problem is basic maths. However, people also misunderstand how probability works as a prediction tool. They don't understand variables and the degree to which they're dependent.

P: OK ...

T: If you had just thrown a head, or indeed six heads or ten, the probability of the next throw being a head is still 50%, not 25% or smaller. That's because these are random events out of your control. However, the probability of having a heart attack, say, is dependent on whether you've had one before. If you have, the risk of another is greatly increased.

P: Time to cut down on salt!

T: Well, maybe, but claims about direct correlations also need to be treated sceptically. As an extreme comparison, the fact that TV sales may increase in line with crime does not prove that one affects the other!

P: Well, you're beginning to convince me, but can you give some other examples ...

▶ TRACK 23

Story 1
The main issue here is that it's difficult to interpret this story without knowing the number of accidents per journey or mile travelled. If there were twice as many journeys in fair weather, then the snowstorm has indeed led to an increase in the accident rate. Really, you'd need more evidence over a period of time to fully establish a correlation between accidents and weather. It could be that bad weather really does reduce incidents due to people driving more carefully.

Story 2
The statistics themselves in this study were accurately collected and described. However, the lobby group who commissioned the study were so-called 'stay-at-home mums', and in the interpretation and the narrow time frame of the study, there was a strong element of twisting the data to fit a conclusion they'd set out to find.

The truth, which was ignored in the analysis, is that aggression is a normal developmental stage in which children test boundaries. Not only is aggression normal, it doesn't usually last. The study failed to measure the stay-at-home toddlers' behaviour when they were mixed in groups, where the same levels of aggression can be observed. Indeed, a follow-up study by different researchers discovered that those kids who had been kept at home exhibited more aggression later at school than those who'd been in nursery, i.e. it simply appeared at a later stage.

Story 3
This statistic seems counterintuitive, but only if you ignore other evidence. The study fails to mention that the number of fatalities dropped dramatically. As more people survive accidents, more are treated for injury. Of course, the statistic as it stands also tells us nothing about the severity of the injuries.

Story 4
The group was self-selecting so we might imagine those strongly against animal testing would be more likely to take part, and there's already probably a bias in terms of the readership of the magazine. Furthermore, the poll was actually conducted following a news report on cruelty and mistreatment in one laboratory.

Story 5
The base numbers are all true. However, the starting point that was chosen was the year when there had been a terrorist bombing in the city, which obviously inflated the figures. In previous years, the figures had actually been 94 and 98. Of course, whether any fall in murders can be attributed to government policy is another thing. There could be a number of underlying causes.

UNIT 8

▶ TRACK 24

1

A: Is that you there?

B: Yeah.

A: Where is that? It looks pretty high up.

B: It was in the Dolomites. It's a range in northern Italy. That peak was about 3,000 metres, I think.

A: Wow! The view from up there must've been pretty breathtaking!

B: Yeah, it was stunning, it really was.

A: So, was there a cable car, or something?

B: Cable car! What? You don't think I'm fit enough to climb up?

A: No, no, it's not that. It's just that it looks pretty terrifying. I mean, that's a proper rocky ridge.

B: Yeah, it looks a bit worse than it actually was, to be honest, and there are these fixed metal ropes that you can clip yourself onto. I mean, it's a bit of a scramble, but you don't need any great technical expertise. You can more or less just pull yourself up the worst bits.

A: Really? I'm not sure I'd trust some rusty old cables.

B: No, they're fairly secure. I mean, you need a head for heights, but it's fine. It's not like these guys we saw base jumping.

A: What?

B: You know what it is, yeah? Where they just throw themselves off a cliff and parachute down?

A: Yeah, yeah. It's nuts.

B: I know! We saw people doing it. I mean, all round that area there are these peaks and deep gorges with these incredible sheer cliffs and we watched some guys jump off one in these kind of flying suits.

A: They must have a death wish, those people, they really must.

B: There are videos of them all on YouTube – just search Dolomites and base jumping.

A: Wugh! It gives me the fear just thinking about it!

2

C: Who's that, then?

D: Oh, that's my uncle and cousins ... and that's me.

C: Uh? Oh yeah! How old are you there?

D: I must've been seven or eight, I guess.

C: So where is that?

D: Mauritius. My dad's from there originally and there was a family reunion.

C: Really? So where is Mauritius?

D: It's basically a tropical island in the Indian Ocean.

C: Wow! I was gonna say – you look like you're in a jungle.

D: Yeah, I think it's a national park. There are some more photos if you flick through.

C: Wow! Look at that! Is that a waterfall there?

D: Yeah. That's where we went. I think it might be an old volcanic crater. I'm not sure, I might be making that up.

C: What? And you walked through that?

D: Yeah. They've already hacked trails through it so it's not that hard. I mean, anywhere else and it's really thick dense jungle. You really have to stick to the tracks.

C: Aww. Look at him there in this one, looking all upset.

D: Alright, alright. There's no need to take the mickey. You would've been a bit freaked-out if you'd just been attacked by some creepy-crawly.

C: Aww! Shame. You poor thing.

D: Yeah, yeah. Actually, my mum said I moaned pretty much incessantly on that trip.

C: Oh gosh! Yeah! You look miserable there too, you really do! How can you not be happy there? Look at that. White sand, crystal clear water, palm trees. What's wrong with you? It's like paradise. It's amazing.

D: I was a little English boy, wasn't I? It was too hot. And there's scorpions and snakes and jellyfish and stuff. I was missing home!

C: Man, I'd love to go there, I really would.

D: Yeah, well, I'd probably appreciate it more now.

C: You haven't been there since?

D: Nah, can't afford it. Dad said he spent years in debt from that trip! Hopefully, one day, though.

▶ TRACK 25

1 I wouldn't drive it if I were you, I really wouldn't.
2 The views were just stunning, they really were.
3 The scenery takes your breath away, it really does.
4 I just love it there, I really do.
5 It made no difference whatsoever, it really didn't.
6 He'll never change, he really won't.
7 I've never been anywhere like it, I really haven't.
8 That sounds amazing, it really does.

▶ TRACK 26

It's common knowledge that men and women do things differently, isn't it? The male of the species, we're told, goes quiet and retreats into a cave to brood at the slightest sign of stress, whilst the female reaches out and shares her feelings. After all, women are better communicators, aren't they? That's certainly what writers like John Gray would have us believe, but on what basis do they make this argument? And does it matter?

It's easy to assume these books must be based on valid scientific research, but in reality very few are. Indeed, even a cursory inspection of the literature of linguistics and gender reveals that men and women communicate in remarkably similar ways. Take the notion that women talk more. A book in 2007 reported that women used 20,000 words a day and men just 7,000, but when the claim was challenged, the author, Louann Brizendine, couldn't provide a source and promised to withdraw it from later editions. In fact, research in the journal Science has shown both sexes talk equally as much, and in doing so use on average 16,000 words per day. There's obviously huge variety – from 500 to 45,000 words a day – but significantly, the three chattiest people in the study were all men!

Then there's the belief that men interrupt more because they are biologically more aggressive and programmed to use language more competitively. Evidence from Janet Hyde actually suggests that in neutral situations, where people speak on equal terms, women and men interrupt equally. The neutrality of the situation is important. Some men do speak over others more, but this is not to do with gender but rather the power relationship between the speakers. When talking to a boss we won't butt in, but they will. In fact, when Chambers reviewed a number of linguistic studies investigating gender difference in this and other areas such as empathising, aggression and wordplay, he found an overlap of 99.75% in the way the sexes communicate. In short, no difference whatsoever!

Finally, if these supposed language differences were biological, we would expect them to be universal to all cultures. However, to take just one example, a study in the village of Gapun, Papua New Guinea, found the men pride themselves on their ability to speak indirectly and never say what they mean, while the women frequently give voice to their anger by launching into lengthy swearing sessions – behaviour which is a reversal of the Mars and Venus stereotypes of aggression and indirectness.

So, why do these myths of biological difference and communication persist? Well, sweeping generalisations such as 'Women are more in touch with their feelings' appeal because they match longstanding stereotypes. We look for and cite evidence to back up a traditional view, but ignore or fail to search for contradictory evidence! Take the psychologist Simon Baron-Cohen, who argues in his book The Essential Difference that male brains are analytical and goal-orientated, which makes them wonderful scientists and lawyers; while the female's empathetic brain is best for jobs like teaching and counselling.

However, as Deborah Cameron notes, a career in education or as a therapist just requires a mix of verbal, people and analytical skills, and Baron-Cohen's choice is simply based on the fact jobs in such fields have traditionally been occupied by women. And why have they? Because they're less well paid, less varied, and have less power in a society that has been dominated by men for centuries. Furthermore, all of this is often reinforced by our biased use of language, where we'll still often specify a *male* nurse or a *female* doctor.

Ultimately then, when, when and how people communicate has far more to do with social status and power than it does with genetic make-up and nature. It's vital to challenge these myths because, in many cases, stereotypes around gender and communication serve to hide the structural problems in societies that maintain male power and hold back women.

▶ TRACK 27

1

Unusually for this species, it can swim underwater as well as tunnel underground, which is handy as it inhabits low wetland areas. Its long claws are adapted for tunnelling through the earth and its water-resistant fur allows it to remain underwater. The long thick tail is thought to store extra fat to draw upon during the mating season. The mole is functionally blind, which is why it has developed the distinctive star-shaped set of feelers that give it its name. These feelers allow it to sense nearby movement.

Uniquely, the mole can also smell underwater. It does this by blowing out tiny bubbles through its nose in order to capture scents that are sucked back in. These adaptations are highly efficient and the star-nosed mole is apparently the fastest eater in the animal kingdom, being able to identify, snatch and consume its prey all in a matter of milliseconds.

2

While the sparrow hawk is more commonly found in woodland, its short broad wings and long tail allow it to manoeuvre quickly through the trees, while the light striped markings on its breast and its darker upper parts help it to blend into the background, as it tends to lie in wait for its prey before shooting out. It has relatively long legs that enable it to kill in mid-flight. The long slender central toe is adapted to grasp, while a small projection on the underside of the claw enables it to grip and hold onto its prey whilst flying. Its small hooked beak is used for plucking and tearing flesh rather than killing. It also sometimes hunts on foot through vegetation. In recent years, it has appeared more and more in cities, where it has no predators and where it is often seen as a pest, damaging garden bird populations.

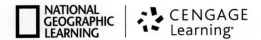

Outcomes Advanced
Student's Book Split A

Hugh Dellar and Andrew Walkley

Publisher: Gavin McLean

Publishing Consultant: Karen Spiller

Development Editor: Katy Wright

Editorial Manager: Claire Merchant

Head of Strategic Marketing ELT: Charlotte Ellis

Senior Content Project Manager: Nick Ventullo

Senior Production Controller: Eyvett Davis

Cover design: emc design

Text design: Alex Dull

Compositor: emc design

National Geographic Liaison: Leila Hishmeh

Audio: Tom Dick & Debbie Productions Ltd

DVD: Tom Dick & Debbie Productions Ltd

Student's Book Split A ISBN: 978-1-337-56126-6

National Geographic Learning
Cheriton House
North Way
Andover
UK
SP10 5BE

Cengage Learning is a leading provider of customized learning solutions with employees residing in nearly 40 different countries and sales in more than 125 countries around the world. Find your local representative at **www.cengage.com**.

Cengage Learning products are represented in Canada by Nelson Education Ltd.

Visit National Geographic Learning online at **ngl.cengage.com**
Visit our corporate website at **www.cengage.com**

Printed in Greece by Bakis SA
Print Number: 01   Print Year: 2017

CREDITS

Although every effort has been made to contact copyright holders before publication, this has not always been possible. If contacted, the publisher will undertake to rectify any errors or omissions at the earliest opportunity.

Photos

6–7 © Paul Nicklen/National Geographic Creative; 8 © R. Hackenberg/Corbis; 10 (l) © nito/Shutterstock.com; 10 (r) © Raymond Patrick/National Geographic Creative; 11 © Mark Lovatt/Getty Images; 12 © Chris Bickford/National Geographic Creative; 14–15 © ZUMA Press, Inc/Alamy Stock Photo; 16 (tl) © Paul Bradbury/Getty Images; 16 (tm) © Alan Powdrill/Getty Images; 16 (tr) © Don Mason/Getty Images; 16 (bl) © Roger Wright/Getty Images; 16 (bm) © Adam Berry/Stringer/Getty Images; 16 (br) © UniversalImagesGroup/Getty Images; 17 (t) © Emmanuel Faure/Getty Images; 17 (b) © ullstein bild/Getty Images; 18–19 © Fritz Hoffmann/National Geographic Creative; 20 © Randy Belice/Getty Images; 22 © Alex Treadway/National Geographic Creative; 24–25 © Sean Gallup/Getty Images; 26 © Cory Richards/National Geographic Creative; 29 © Tomaz Levstek/Getty Images; 30 (tl) © Peter Evans/Alamy Stock Photo; 30 (tr) © Jim Richardson/National Geographic Creative; 30 (bl) © Jack Sullivan/Alamy Stock Photo; 30 (br) © Mark Runnacles/Stringer/Getty Images; 31 (t) © Cate Gillon/Getty Images; 31 (b) © Matthew Taylor/Alamy Stock Photo; 32–33 © Lou Avers/dpa/Corbis; 34 © Daniel Roland/AFP/Getty Images; 37 © EMPPL PA Wire/Associated Press/AP Images; 38–39 © Arnd Wiegmann/Reuters/Corbis; 40 © Frans Lanting/National Geographic Creative; 42–43 © Oso Media/Alamy Stock Photo; 44 © MASSIVE/Getty Images; 45 © Yadid Levy/Alamy Stock Photo; 47 (t) © Richard Newstead/Getty Images; 47 (bl) © Miles Willis/Stringer/Getty Images; 47 (br) © Oliver Knight/Alamy Stock Photo; 48 © Victoria Pearson/Getty Images; 49 The Hunger Games. Text copyright © Suzanne Collins, 2008. Reproduced by permission of Scholastic Ltd. All rights reserved.; 50–51 © Joel Sartore/National Geographic Creative; 52 © Bill Whitehead/Cartoonstock; 53 © Bill Whitehead/Cartoonstock; 54 © Ed Darack/Getty Images; 55 © Chris Hopkins/Stringer/Getty Images; 56 © Phil Walter/Getty Images; 58 © Yury Dmitrienko/Shutterstock.com; 60–61 © Mark Thiessen/National Geographic Creative; 62 © Rick & Nora Bowers/Alamy Stock Photo; 65 © Photos 12 / Alamy Stock Photo; 66 © Fran/Cartoonstock; 67 © Glenn and Gary McCoy/Cartoonstock; 68–69 © Michael Nichols/National Geographic Creative; 71 (t) © Bill Hatcher/National Geographic Creative; 71 (b) © Bruno Kolberg/EyeEm/Getty Images; 73 © David Burch/Getty Images; 74 (tl) © MVPhoto/Shutterstock.com; 74 (tml) © Thomas Marent/Visuals Unlimited/Corbis; 74 (tmr) © Colin Monteath/Hedgehog House/Getty Images; 74 (tr) © Mark Medcalf/Shutterstock.com; 74 (bl) © Roderick Paul Walker/Alamy Stock Photo; 74 (bml) © Ken Catania/Visuals Unlimited/Corbis; 74 (bmr) © dexterous simpson/Shutterstock.com; 74 (br) © Kevin Schafer/Alamy Stock Photo; 76 © STR/Reuters/Corbis; 80 © Stoyan Yotov/Shutterstock.com; 83 © Paul Brown/Demotix/Corbis; 85 © Franco Origlia/Getty Images; 95 © Raymond Patrick/National Geographic Creative; 96 © Mark Lovatt/Getty Images; 99 © javarman/Shutterstock.com; 100 (tl) © Worldpics/Shutterstock.com; 100 (tr) © Anton_Ivanov/Shutterstock.com; 100 (bl) © Ammit Jack/Shutterstock.com; 100 (bm) © Alexandra Lande/Shutterstock.com; 100 (br) © pavel dudek/Shutterstock.com; 101 © nito/Shutterstock.com.

Cover

Cover photograph © Henry Sudarman/500px.

Illustrations

70 Martin Sanders/Beehive Illustration; 84 KJA Artists.

Acknowledgements

The publishers and authors would like to thank the following teachers who provided the feedback and user insights on the first edition of *Outcomes* that have helped us develop this new edition: Rosetta d'Agostino, New English Teaching, Milan, Italy; Victor Manuel Alarcón, EOI Badalona, Badalona, Spain; Isidro Almendarez, Universidad Complutense, Madrid, Spain; Ana Bueno Amaro, EOI Roquetas de Mar, Almería, Spain; Isabel Andrés, EOI Valdemoro, Madrid, Spain; Brian Brennan, International House Company Training, Barcelona, Spain; Nara Carlini, Università Cattolica, Milan, Italy; Karen Corne, UK; Jordi Dalmau, EOI Reus, Reus, Spain; Matthew Ellman, British Council, Malaysia; Clara Espelt, EOI Maresme, Barcelona, Spain; Abigail Fulbrook, Chiba, Japan; Dylan Gates, Granada, Spain; Blanca Gozalo, EOI Fuenlabrada, Madrid, Spain; James Grant, Japan; Joanna Faith Habershon, St Giles Schools of Languages London Central, UK; Jeanine Hack; English Language Coach.com, London, UK; Claire Hart, Germany; David Hicks, Languages4Life, Barcelona, Spain; Hilary Irving, Central School of English, London, UK; Jessica Jacobs, Università Commerciale Luigi Bocconi, Milan, Italy; Lucia Luciani, Centro di Formaziones Casati, Milan, Italy; Izabela Michalak, ELC, Łódz´, Poland; Josep Millanes Moya, FIAC Escola d'Idiomes, Terrassa, Catalonia; Rodrigo Alonso Páramo, EOI Viladecans, Barcelona, Spain; Jonathan Parish, Uxbridge College, London, UK; Mercè Falcó Pegueroles, EOI Tortosa, Tortosa, Spain; Hugh Podmore, St Giles Schools of Languages London Central, UK; James Rock, Università Cattolica, Milan, Italy; Virginia Ron, EOI Rivas, Madrid, Spain; Coletto Russo, British Institutes, Milan, Italy; Ana Salvador, EOI Fuenlabrada, Madrid, Spain; Adam Scott, St Giles College, Brighton, UK; Olga Smolenskaya, Russia; Carla Stroulger, American Language Academy, Madrid, Spain; Simon Thomas, St Giles, UK; Simon Thorley, British Council, Madrid, Spain; Helen Tooke, Università Commerciale Luigi Bocconi, Milan, Italy; Chloe Turner, St Giles Schools of Languages London Central, UK; Sheila Vine, University of Paderborn, Germany; Richard Willmsen, British Study Centres, London, UK; Various teachers at English Studio Academic management, UK.

Authors' acknowledgements

Thanks to Karen Spiller and Katy Wright, and to Dennis Hogan, John McHugh and Gavin McLean for their continued support and enthusiasm.

Thanks also to all the students we've taught over the years for providing more inspiration and insight than they ever realised.

And to the colleagues we've taught alongside for their friendship, thoughts and assistance.